From Surviving to Thriving

Change Your Energy,
Change Your Life

Mark Lorentzen

D1468623

From Surviving to Thriving:
Change Your Energy, Change Your Life

Copyright 2005 by Mark Lorentzen

All rights reserved. This publication may not be reproduced, stored in a retrieval system, or transmitted in whole or in part, in any form or by any means, electronic, mechanical, photocopying, recording, or otherwise without the prior written permission of the author.

For information, contact Puma Publications www. pumapublications.com

Edited by Linda Jay Geldens – www.lindajaygeldens.com
Illustrations by Hogie McMurtry – www.hogiemcmurtry.com
Interior design and layout by Robert Goodman, Silvercat™– rg@silvercat.com
Cover design and layout by ThreeBears.com
Cover coordination by Meredith Gould – www.meredithgould.com

Publisher's Cataloging-in-Publication
(Provided by Quality Books, Inc.)

Lorentzen, Mark.
    From surviving to thriving : change your energy, change your life / Mark Lorentzen.
        p. cm.
    Includes bibliographical references.
    ISBN 0-9748268-0-4

    1. Change (Psychology) 2. Self-actualization (Psychology) 3. Mind and body.   I. Title.

BF637.C4L67 2005   158.1
                             QBI04-800056

Printed in the United States of America

Contents

This book is dedicated to my dear father,
who lovingly encouraged me to follow my dreams

He died two days after
I finished writing this book

Acknowledgments

While there have been so many co-journeyers along my path, there are a few that I would like to mention by name who are part of my spiritual family. My deepest gratitude goes to Marcela Flekalova and Bruce Sweatte, both master healers and teachers. Their love, light, and continuous faith in me held the space to write this book. Whenever I was truly stuck, they had the answers. There never would have been a book without my soul-brother Ralph Parnefjord. He convinced me that the chakras were real and not just a philosophical idea. My compañiero Mike Kass was there through many of the big experiences that shaped me. Thank you for hashing out all of the issues in a humorous and loving manner — and for your insistence that we have a greater calling. My deep appreciation to Bo Milan for his belief in me, and for giving me my first break as a teacher at his Natural Success School for Holistics. My gratitude to Matt Lynch for his support, humor, wisdom, and demonstration of commitment. I'd like to give a special thank you to Kimberly Alkema. Although we have parted ways, she was part of my inspiration. I've been blessed to have all these wonderful beings in my life.

I've also been very fortunate to have gifted teachers, starting with my first therapist Dr. Tom Rusk. Along with helping me resolve many of my own issues, he was a great philosophical resource and is referenced several times in this book. My appreciation goes to the faculty at Pacifica Graduate Institute, who live up to their motto of "tending the soul of the world." Words can not express how grateful I am to Victoria and Gordon Merkle for their healing energy and loving guidance. I attended their healing school while writing my manuscript, so much of what I've written of my experiences occurred in tandem with their teaching. My gratitude to Carolyn Myss for her pioneering efforts and courage in getting chakras into mainstream consciousness, along with a special thank you for her permission to share some of her words of wisdom. My appreciation to Rosalyn Bruyere, a teacher of teachers, whose gems of wisdom went to the core of several of my issues. A big thank you to Craig Junjulas for helping me to listen to my intuition and to *see* beyond the ordinary world. A special thank you to Marianne Williamson for allowing me to reprint her verse.

A tremendous thank you to all of the people who helped me put this book together. First and foremost, my editor Linda Jay Geldens, who helped to make the text crisper and easier to understand (all of you readers should thank her). Her suggestions extended beyond rewriting sections to organizing the ideas better. A glimpse of my original manuscript would show you the difference she made. I'd also like to thank another soul-brother, Chuck Tedesco, for his preliminary editing of my rough draft. Special thanks to Joe Liddy for catchingall the mistakes in the final proofreading. A big appreciation for the talents of Hogie McMurtry for his wonderful illustrations. I'd like to extend my gratitude to Bob Goodman for the layout of this book, making it organized and beautiful. A special thank you to Meredith Gould and Paul Schindel for their amazing skill in creating the front and rear cover. And finally, appreciation to Penny Sansevieri for getting me in contact with many of the people I just mentioned. As the organizer of my publicity, her contribution is just starting.

Introduction

Inspiration

We live in a unique and exciting era. Never before in history has there been so much information available for personal and spiritual growth. Many sacred teachings that were lost — or hidden away in mystery schools — have now been brought back to light and are accessible to the general population. New information is being collected at a remarkable rate and being spread rapidly. Additionally, there are a great number of facilitators present with sophisticated techniques to guide and assist people in psychospiritual growth. As individuals and collectively, we are on the doorstep of new possibilities, capable of making great leaps and changes. Are you ready to embrace the future in a loving and courageous manner?

My experiences have led me to a deep exploration of what helps people to move forward in their lives and why some people remain stuck. Rather than work exclusively with individuals in a one-on-one setting, I was inspired to share the information that I have gathered through a series of books and workshops. This is part of my overall mission to facilitate collective progress through individual growth. I espouse no specific religious dogma or political agenda in this book; rather, I simply suggest some ideas that may help you. Trust your own discernment to sort out what is true for yourself. As a byproduct of personal empowerment, like-minded people will naturally gather for mutually beneficial projects that have increasingly enlightened intentions. Perhaps in the near future, all humans will recognize our common bond as denizens of the earth, engendering a spirit of cooperation, and learning to work together in harmony.

A few thoughts on energy

You experience energy every day in forms such as electricity, light, sound, and heat. Since Einstein's famous equation, $E=mc^2$, science has learned a great deal about the nature of energy. For example, we know that light can behave like a particle or a vibratory wave. When viewed on a minute and elemental scale, everything is made up of energy. Objects are made of various substances that are made of molecules, which in turn are made of protons, neutrons, and electrons (which are made of even smaller quarks). The smaller the scale, the more difficult it is to distinguish between particles and energy.

The amount of space that is occupied by a *solid* proton is very small in comparison to the overall size of a hydrogen atom: almost all of the atom is empty space. The point is that physical objects are not really as solid as they appear to be.

Finally, your consciousness can affect energy. Many studies have shown that a scientist's or a participant's expectation will affect the outcome of experiments — whether examining the interface between particles and energy or the roll of dice. Energy and consciousness both have vibratory waves and patterns. Since these terms describe different aspects of the same phenomenon, they will be used almost interchangeably in this book.

Sensing energy

Popular culture is full of phrases like "that place had good energy" or "I got bad vibes from that person." These are not technical descriptions of energy or vibration, but rather an overall sense or feeling that you experience. We are always sensing energies, although most often not consciously. For example, if a person were to come into your workplace, walk around, and leave without saying anything, you would have an impression of him or her regarding comfort and trust. But how are you sure, without the person ever having said a word? Because you can sense the person's energy!

I encourage you to suspend your disbelief while you are reading this book and trying the exercises that I describe. Energy has many forms and vibrations. The average human can hear only a certain range of tones. Dogs have a higher range of hearing than humans. Dog whistles are audible to dogs, but not to humans. Bats navigate according to sonar. The average human can see a range of visible light, beyond which is infrared and ultraviolet light. Just because you cannot see or hear various forms of energy does not mean that they do not exist. Indeed, there are many ranges of energetic vibration used to identify physical objects, such as X rays and radar, which you would never question.

It is possible to feel your own energy. Hold your hands about ten inches apart, with your palms facing each other. Slowly bring them toward each other, without touching. As your hands get closer, you will feel them drawn together like a magnet. At this point, stop and move your hands apart about an inch and notice the difference (Figures 1 and 2). Can you feel the pressure between your hands? After you have sensed this energy between your hands, move them back and forth as if you were playing an accordion. How far can you pull your hands apart and still feel the energy between them?

While almost everyone can sense their energy in the above exercise, fewer people can see their own energy. Try holding your hands in front of your face about ten inches from your eyes, with your fingertips

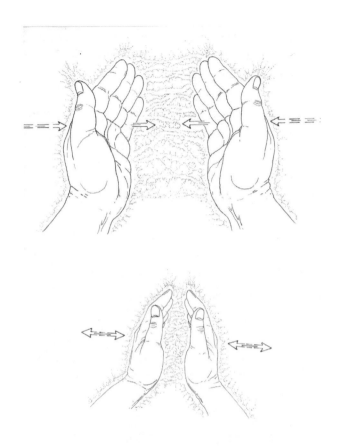

Figures 1 and 2: Sensing energy

toward each other. Bring your fingertips about half an inch from each other. Look at the space between your fingertips (Figures 3 and 4). Can you see the clear or light blue energy that looks like heat waves? You can play with this by moving one of your hands up and down and noticing the difference.

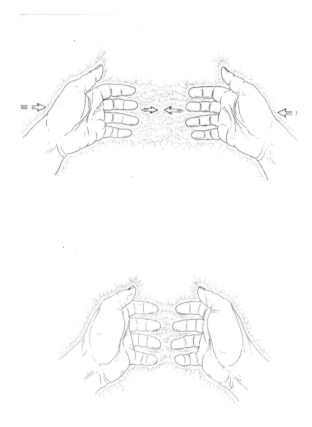

Figures 3 and 4: Seeing energy

Now quickly breathe in and out, taking in five deep breaths. How do you feel? What do you notice about your energy? If you try the exercises again, you should have an easier time sensing your increased energy. You can also try quickly rubbing your hands together to increase energy.

Do you notice a difference? Was it easier to feel or see your energy?

Energy psychology

Energy psychology is a new field that has recently emerged. It combines the understanding of psychology with effective energetic healing techniques. This is a natural marriage, as psychology grew from a mental and emotional approach to include the body and spirit, while energetic healing approaches embraced psychology in order to help integrate new behaviors based on energetic changes.

Energy psychology divides the human energy system into three main categories:

- Energy pathways — used in acupuncture, shiatsu massage, tapping, and reflexology
- Energetic biosphere or aura
- Seven main energy centers or *chakras*

The word chakra means wheel or disk in Sanskrit. But just because it was first described in India does not make the chakra system a purely Indian concept, any more than your liver might be considered German if it had been labeled first by a German doctor. Livers and chakras existed long before they were identified and named. It is also not necessary to buy into the belief that these energy centers exist for you to get something out of this book. They can also be viewed as metaphors, archetypes, an interesting theory — or you can simply ignore the framework and use the practical suggestions as they apply to you.

Many clairvoyant healers, however, can see and work directly with these chakras, considering them a matter of fact rather than a belief.

While chakras have been around for a long time, the sophistication of psychology that was needed to describe and understand the phenomenon is a relatively new development. With the birth of energy psychology, more studies will be performed, which will generate more detailed information. No more than forty books have been written in English on the chakras and almost all of these books have been *introductions to the chakras.* This is the first book to focus exclusively on the root chakra. Check out my website — www.allaboutchoice.net — for future updates about my books on the other six chakras.

My intention is to translate my experiences and knowledge into clear everyday language, along with presenting a practical approach to psychospiritual growth. In this way, I hope to demystify the chakra system and make these concepts accessible to all.

The seven chakras or energy centers

Each chakra takes energy in, records your experience, and distributes energy. Clairvoyants describe the chakras as energy vortexes that spin. When a chakra is blocked or distorted in some manner, this affects your ability to take energy into your system (Figures 5 and 6).

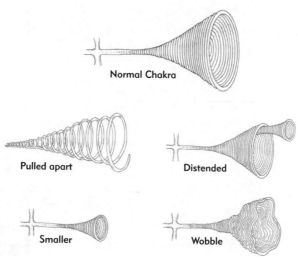

Normal Chakra

Pulled apart

Distended

Smaller

Wobble

Figure 5: Normal chakra and some distortions

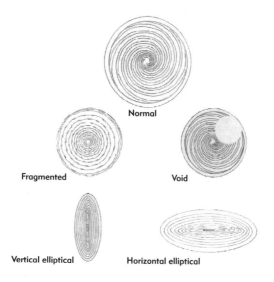

Normal

Fragmented

Void

Vertical elliptical

Horizontal elliptical

Figure 6: Normal chakra, "head on" view, with distortions

While you have many smaller energy centers or chakras, we will focus on the seven main chakras. They have the following locations (Figure 7):

- Crown chakra: centered just above your head, with the wide end up
- Third eye chakra: centered between your eyebrows
- Throat chakra: center of your throat
- Heart chakra: center of your chest, parallel to your physical heart
- Solar plexus chakra: centered just below your rib cage
- Sacral chakra: centered just below — and including — your belly button
- Root chakra: centered between your legs, with the wide end down

With the exception of your crown and root chakras, each chakra has both a front and back side (Figure 8).

Each chakra is like a separate universe that represents a discrete state of consciousness, with a characteristic color and energetic vibration. Like rungs on a ladder, there is a jump from one chakra to the next. I have given the energy and consciousness of each chakra a descriptive label, along with an easy to identify phrase that characterizes its perspective. These phrases are the language that you often use to talk about and justify your choices at each chakra. This

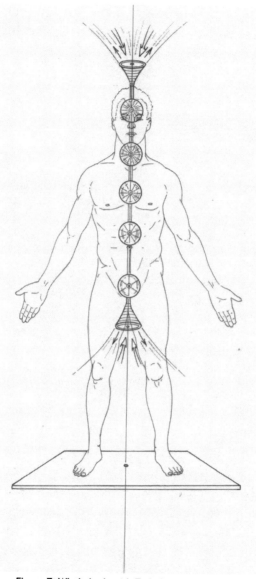

Figure 7: Whole body with 7 chakras (front view)

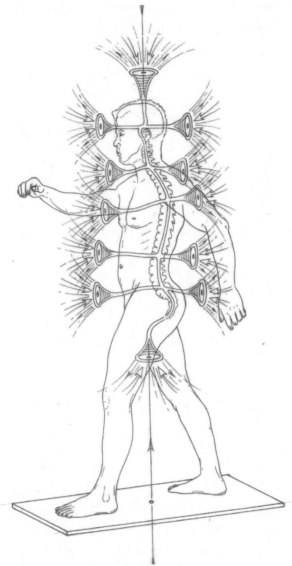

Figure 8: Whole body with 7 chakras (side view)

reflects your internal programming, which is a powerful influence in shaping your experience of the world, often becoming a self-fulfilling prophecy.

The general development of your chakras

Everyone has these seven chakras, which are all functioning to some extent all of the time. Ideally, all of your chakras would be wide open and well-functioning, as each chakra serves a vital function. No one chakra is better or more important than another. Indeed, living a balanced life requires that you develop all of them. It is also advantageous to be able to operate from a specific chakra when a situation calls for it; drawing on the qualities of that energy. For example, a jazz musician would be well-served to have access to the creative energy and expressive consciousness of his throat chakra while playing music. However, he might benefit from having access to the strategic consciousness of his solar plexus chakra when making his schedule — or accessing his personal power when negotiating his contracts.

Each chakra has a primary developmental period. Your root chakra is the first to develop, then your sacral chakra, and so on. However, life does not always follow such a linear path and all of your chakras are constantly taking in energy and recording your experiences. If you miss a step in your development, you can revisit it at a later time. There is usually one chakra from which you operate most of the time, that corresponds to your overall stage of psychospiritual development.

The root chakra is the densest energy and is where you will experience the greatest sense of limitation. As your development moves up toward the crown chakra, you will experience less density, an expanded sense of choice, and greater freedom. Shifting your consciousness to a higher chakra requires taking more responsibility — since freedom, choice, and responsibility are inseparably linked.

When you have established a sense of security, you can begin to develop at the sacral chakra, pursuing experiences that give you pleasure. The focus also shifts from group consciousness to one-on-one relationships, with an emphasis on your emotions.

Empowering your solar plexus chakra requires a big shift, as you let go of codependent behavior and victim consciousness (in which others are always to blame). This is a movement toward independence, personal accountability, and gaining control over the direction of your life. You have to claim this step, as no one can do it for you.

Opening your heart chakra involves a radical reversal; from a focus on control to being vulnerable, open, and willing to view a situation from another person's perspective. As part of this major change, your choices now become based on love rather than fear. You begin to go beyond yourself, having empathy and compassion for others.

Crown Chakra — Purple turning to White

Divine Energy / Cosmic or Unity Consciousness
"Experiencing connection with everything here and now."

Third Eye Chakra — Indigo

Shamanic Energy / Contemplative Consciousness
"I'm aligned with my higher intention to..."

Throat Chakra — Blue

Creative Energy / Expressive Consciousness
I joyfully flow with..."

Heart Chakra — Green

Loving Energy / Compassionate Consciousness
"I love to..."

Solar Plexus Chakra — Yellow

Personal Power Energy / Strategic Consciousness
"I want to..."

Sacral Chakra — Orange

Emotional-Sexual Energy / Relational Consciousness
"You should or ought to do this..."

Root Chakra — Red

Tribal Energy / Survival or Security Consciousness
"You have or need to do this..."

Developing your throat chakra continues the trend of letting go of control so that you can flow with events as they unfold naturally. However, this is not blind surrender, but occurs as you tune into and follow your personal guidance while owning responsibility for what you co-create. This is a purposeful and inventive approach to life that views every event as an opportunity. It results in an attitude of gratitude for the lessons that you learn and the joyful times that you experience.

Developing your third eye chakra involves being able to detach from your emotions and quiet the chatter of your mind, so that you can perceive reality with greater clarity. This extends to cultivating an awareness of your patterns of projection and denial. Eventually, even your secondary or negative intentions are owned. Your life becomes much more intentional as you cultivate the ability to change your patterns.

Experiencing life from your crown chakra translates to a present time awareness, focusing on what is happening *here and now* (with no thoughts of the past or expectations of the future). Living life from unity consciousness involves transcending any kind of separation, allowing a direct connection to your Higher Self and God. This is often associated with mystical experiences. In everyday life, you can picture your crown chakra like the operating system of a computer, seen in the principles and values that you live by.

We are constantly moving from one energy to the next. As you move up the chakras, you are generally going from a physical experience to working through your emotions and related thoughts, so that you can own your experience and eventually let go or merge with it. When you are moving down the chakras, you are generally taking an inspiration, translating it into a creative idea, and then integrating it as a new pattern in your life or manifesting the idea in a physical form.

The goal is to have access to all of your chakras, so that you are not stuck in any particular pattern, but have the conscious option of choosing which chakra to operate from. Then, when you experience difficulties, you can explore if another perspective might produce a more beneficial outcome. This results in greater freedom of choice. For example, even visionary third eye leaders still enjoy the creativity of their throat chakra, retain the empathy of their heart chakra, maintain their solar plexus chakra ability to make specific plans, can feel the emotions of their sacral chakra, and take care of the physical needs of their root chakra. However, these other activities are no longer their main focus and do not rule their lives.

The role of choice

Choice is the gift and the fundamental power of the human experience.
Caroline Myss

At each chakra you make choices, which is how energy gets distributed. Your energy then affects the endocrine glands and nerve centers that are associated with each chakra. You can make great changes in your life by making important choices. It's all about choice!

I believe that every person has free will and that everyone is capable of making difficult, watershed choices to empower themselves. In any case, change is inevitable. You can either go forward in a conscious and courageous manner, or you can experience being dragged and kicked through life. You have choices. In sharing with you the lessons that I have learned, my hope is that your path may be simpler and easier.

Energetic consequences and victim consciousness

If you always do what you always did, you'll always get what you always got.
Anthony Robbins

The energetic consequence of any important choice is that you either gain or lose energy, which results in your feeling energized or drained. All of your choices have consequences, even those that you make ‚unconsciously. Ignorance or continued denial will not protect you forever.

Worse yet, you may disown your sense of choice and personal responsibility. This shows up when you blame someone or something as the cause of your experience. You might say, "Somebody did this *to me*," as if you were completely removed from the situation. You seek solutions that are outside of yourself, wanting others to change first. From this perspective, *power* seems to reside in other people or institutions that are pulling the strings. Inevitably, when something happens that you don't like, you feel victimized. You start to feel sorry for yourself, triggering the common internal message: "Poor me!" When this occurs often enough to become a pattern, then you are caught up in *victim consciousness.* You always have some kind of excuse, which is another way of expressing that you are not responsible.

Generally, people with this attitude have difficulty changing. They complain a lot, but they are not willing to do anything about their situation. They would like someone else to change the situation for them. This perspective tends to keep them stuck in victim consciousness. While this state of mind can often result in many painfully difficult situations, there are reasons why people can get stuck in this mode. Usually, early traumatic experiences have blocked their psychospiritual growth.

I have tremendous empathy and compassion for the difficulties of being human. While I've had some significant personal challenges, many people have experienced much more troubling circumstances than I have. The only thing that any of us can do is to play the cards that we have been dealt in life in the best way we know how.

I get a sense that a massive shift is occurring, as people are having less and less tolerance for victim consciousness and the "poor me" attitude associated with it. Valuable information, effective tools and techniques for psychospiritual growth are available, as well as various forms of guidance and support. So, though moving forward may seem to be a scary venture, the alternative of giving up, quitting, or not attempting is becoming less acceptable. In the prophetic words of Michael Jordan: "I just can't see not trying."

Sadly, the consequences of victim consciousness are potentially more devastating. The attitude of quitting and giving away personal power can become destructive because it blocks your natural flow of energy. Over time, distorted energy patterns can influence the physical tissue of your body. Furthermore, my belief is that victim consciousness is a breeding ground for disease. Grossly simplified, you are giving up energy that may be necessary to combat potential disease states.

We only have so much energy with which to run our lives, and using that energy to run our past more than our present causes us to run into energetic debt. Eventually the resources with which we pay this debt come from the energy in our cell tissue, weakening our body into a condition that allows illness to develop.

Caroline Myss

As the rate of change in the world continues to increase, the challenges will increase also. If you do not actively respond to the ever-changing new realities, then by passively choosing not to respond, you may end up self-selecting: taking yourself out of the game of life by not trying. While this is tough talk, it is not intended to spread fear, but rather to make you face reality. What you are unaware of can still affect you. Do you want to hide like an ostrich with your head in the sand or soar high with the grand perspective of an eagle?

Healing and managing your energy more effectively

My universal vision of growth and healing is grounded in my faith in the ability of the human spirit to overcome any obstacle. The path to healing or improving the quality of your energy begins with your intention to heal: energy follows intention! Of course, to truly heal, you must back up your intentions with actual changes in your behavior.

The second step is to come out of denial and gain greater awareness of your issues. One of the main objectives of this book is to describe the main issues of the root chakra, outlining how the various energetic and behavioral patterns are played out. It is my hope that you will be able to quickly get an understanding of the issues, recognizing both your strengths and your challenges.

The third step is to be more specific by identifying one of your energetic patterns, including drains, distortions, and blocks that limit the flow of your energy. If you track your pattern deeply enough, it is possible to identify the root cause or when it started.

The next step is to own the choices and behaviors that are part of your pattern. This is a major step in your beginning to manage your choices and energy more effectively. If you do not own responsibility for your choices and behaviors, you will not have the full power to make the necessary changes. Everyone wants the freedom to do as they wish. However, true freedom means having the power of choice, not having the absence of responsibility.

This step is followed by releasing (or transmuting) your unwanted energetic pattern, with its associated emotions, thoughts, and beliefs. Sometimes this is simply a process of letting go. If you are dealing with a lifelong pattern, you may need some assistance. There are numerous therapies, including psychology and energetic healing, that are designed to assist you in this step.

After releasing your unwanted energies, you will want to bring in positive energy to replace your old patterns. The last step is to fully integrate new choices and changes in your behavior. If you are making a big change, this process can sometimes take a while, so be patient with yourself as you make courageous choices.

Finally, be grateful for the opportunity afforded you, for the roles that various people have played in your growth, for the lessons learned, for your power to choose, for the greater freedom, and for the abundant, creative universe to which you belong.

Suggestions and disclaimers

This information in this book is educational. It is not intended as a substitute for medical and psychiatric diagnosis or treatment, when needed. Please consult a qualified physician or get psychological counseling for assistance with significant problems.

My intention is that these ideas be used for your personal and spiritual growth. I encourage you to become more aware of your own behavior. Please do not use this model to belittle anyone else by saying, "That is only a root or a sacral chakra choice." If you notice behavior patterns in another person and want to offer a guiding hand, first ask if he would like some feedback. This provides an opening for him to walk through, if he chooses to do so. Make it an offer to come forward without any expectations. Attempting to force others to grow will usually only result in increased resistance and defensiveness.

I also want to make it clear that I do not have all the answers. The model that I present in this book is one way of approaching growth, with concepts that have worked for me, and have had a profound impact on the way I live my life. I encourage you to take what you can use, improve upon my ideas, and find your own creative solutions.

One

Root Chakra

The root chakra is an energy vortex centered at the end of your tailbone. It is red and shaped like a cone, with the pointed top in between your legs and the wide end opening toward the ground (Figures 7 and 8 and also Figures 9 and 10). Its size, rotational speed, color tone, and clarity will depend on your current experience and how far you have evolved with respect to the issues inherent in this energy center. Most people cannot see these energies, so you may have to rely on a self-evaluation as you read through each section of this book (or seek out another person who can give you the necessary feedback).

The root chakra connects you to the earth and all physical experiences. The most important objective of your root chakra is keeping you alive. Almost all issues of this chakra relate to survival, although this connection is usually unconscious in your everyday life. While your root chakra can change and grow throughout your life, the primary developmental period takes place from conception to age two-to-four. At this age, you were dependent on your parents for survival, so many of your root chakra patterns emerged from the dynamics of this early connection.

Your early relationship with your mother was especially important, as she was your main source of food, comfort, and orientation. The quality of this bond was important in establishing an overall sense of security for you and was the basis upon which the rest of your psyche was formed. The extent to which your needs for physical security and nurturing were met made it easier to develop your full potential as you learned how to survive outside the womb as a separate physical self, standing on your own feet. If these needs were not adequately met, then part of your root chakra energy may have been fragmented, blocked, or stuck — setting up psychological hurdles to be overcome later on in life.

In order to understand the mentality of the root chakra, it may be helpful to picture yourself as a two-year-old child. Your ego is just forming and you are very impressionable. You have minimal awareness without much reflection, so your parents' words are taken as the law. Your thinking has an all-or-nothing quality to it. The advantage, as an adult, is that you can become aware of the patterns described in this book which you recognize are your own, but now you can re-parent and coach yourself so that you no longer have to react as a two-year-old.

How are you handling the demands of everyday life? Are you thriving, struggling, or merely surviving? The following list of qualities will help you identify your degree of functioning.

Surviving	**Struggling**	**Thriving**
choice not acknowledged	one choice perceived	adaptable
fundamentalist beliefs	conforming to tribe	your own experience
racist	biased	respects tribal heritage
slave to fear	difficulty trusting	trusting
disconnected	spacy	grounded
disoriented	awkward or confused	well-oriented
overwhelmed, panic, desperate helpless	anxious, vulnerable, worried, nervous	calm, relaxed, centered
sleeping pills	light sleeper	sleeps anywhere
self-destructive	self-sabotaging	has self-worth
alienated	abandoned, lonely	belonging, connection
dependent, abusive	needy, clinging	loyal
sociopath, borderline	borderline traits	stable
every day is a crisis	uncertainty	safe environment

Surviving	Struggling	Thriving
poverty consciousness	on security treadmill	able to care for self
difficulty functioning	difficulty showing up	resilient
victim consciousness	victim traits	projects get done
lethargic	low energy	zest for life
obesity or anorexia	overweight or too thin	athletic
diseases:	weak immune system	vibrant, vitality

chronic lower back pain

osteoporosis

immune system diesases

allergies and environmental sensitivities

cancer in lower colon and rectum

Two

Survival Consciousness

Physical survival is the primary concern of your root chakra. Every experience in which you were scared, felt unsafe, or perceived your survival to be threatened in any manner is recorded in this energy center. This chakra also stores all of the cues that preceded threatening events, as well as your responses that lessened the sense of danger and helped you to cope. In this way, your experience and response patterns are learned so that you can react quickly the next time a similar event is encountered.

While you can be affected by birth experiences as far back as conception, your experience of being separate from your mother as a newborn baby was the basis for much of your survival consciousness. Survival was at stake! You came into the world feeling helpless, extremely vulnerable, and completely dependent on your parents for survival. As a baby, you came into this world with only two basic fears: falling and loud noises. All other fears are learned! So your early experiences taught you which situations were safe and not safe, along with your initial attempts to cope.

Your survival consciousness can also be greatly affected by crisis situations later in life, such as: big accidents, major illnesses, surgery, and wartime experiences. If you have been exposed to any form of traumatic abuse — physical, emotional, and especially sexual — this will also impact your survival consciousness in a powerful way. The point is: whenever you make a choice that is based on what is necessary for survival, you are making a root chakra choice.

Your survival experiences or scariest moments

- What were the most frightening situations you have experienced?
- When have you felt that your life was at stake?
- What have been the biggest crisis situations in your life?
- Did you suffer any abuse as a child?
- What do you know about your mother's pregnancy and your birth?
- What fears did you learn from your parents?
- What have you learned from your survival experiences?

One of my survival experiences

When I do some kind of deep regression therapy, inevitably I connect with experiences that seem to be from the time when I was a fetus in my mother's womb. I had a twin brother who died toward the end of the second trimester, which led to complications during my birth. We were awkwardly arranged side-by-side in the womb. In a modern hospital setting, they would have automatically set up a Caesarian section, but this was a small town in Michigan in 1962. My mother was in labor for three days. At one point, the doctors asked my father, "If we can only save your wife or your baby, who do you want us to save?" Eventually, I was delivered by Caesarian section. My twin had developed to the extent that he was required to have an official burial. The loss of my twin and my first brush with death seem to have been a critical experience, setting up several dynamics that have repeated themselves in various ways throughout my life. For example, I seek relationships that have a closeness similar to a twin connection. Then I play out abandonment scenarios (see the later section on abandonment).

Imprinting

A lot of your root chakra programming took place before you learned language skills, so these patterns were imprinted. Imprinting is a process by which experiences and response patterns are learned and embedded in a highly charged emotional field. Imprinted patterns are recorded biochemically, emotionally, and energetically. As the emotional charge subsides, the imprinted response pattern recedes from awareness into unconscious programming. The imprinted memory then becomes part of your unconscious programming and energetic field. When you encounter a stimulus that is similar to the original imprint, it *triggers* the patterned response that you learned, along with the associated emotions.

The conditioned response of Pavlov's dogs is the most recognizable example. A bell was rung just before the dogs were fed. Within a short time, the dogs began to salivate when the bell was rung, even if it was not followed by food. The bell had become a trigger to salivate. The intensity of your emotional reaction will affect how deeply a pattern becomes imprinted. Dramatic events only need to be experienced once in order to become imprinted in your energetic field, although a less dramatic event which is repeated many times can also leave a strong imprint.

A triggered reaction usually occurs automatically without your awareness and is paralleled by involuntary physiological responses. For example, in states of high stress, your body is put on alert and your adrenal glands start pumping. This is the classic fight, flight, or freeze survival mechanism, which is connected to the primitive, reptilian part of your brain.

Root chakra imprinting is associated with the message:

"If I do not do this, I fear that I will die."

In essence, this programming is replaying the original experience:

I feel threatened, so I react by _____.
If I do not _____, I fear that I will die.

But even though the original threat is no longer present, the programmed behavioral pattern continues. When any threat is perceived as being similar to the original, the unconscious response is acted out, sometimes destructively.

Everyone has many imprinted patterns to which they react. It is just a matter of how intense your reaction is and how quickly you can return to your previous state. You can tell when you are triggered because your response is almost always an *overreaction* to the situation. Triggers can occur several times a day and can result from seemingly trivial incidents. It is common to be triggered in situations where a bit of stress is already present, such as in rush-hour traffic.

Along with genetic inheritance, your imprinted patterns become the basis for your drives, urges, and impulses.

Your triggers

- Which situations do you overreact to?
- What are some of your triggers?
- What will get your adrenaline pumping?
- How do you respond to physical confrontation or intense arguments?
- When triggered, do you tend to fight, flee, or freeze?
- What drives you in life?
- When do your impulses and urges surface?

Uncovering your imprinted patterns

An interchangeable term for imprinting is *state-dependent-learning* — a memory that is connected to the emotional state you were in when you originally experienced it. Re-accessing such a memory requires being in similar emotional state. This means that to truly relearn and rework a deep imprint requires accessing a similar emotional and/or energetic intensity that was present when the imprint was learned (which sometimes results in a spontaneous age regression to the time of the original experience). Because of this, talking about these patterns will not be enough. Early imprints are even more difficult to access, since they were learned before you had language skills.

You will know that you have accessed the survival imprinting of the first level when you encounter your flight, fight, or freeze mechanism. This can come up in daily life when a situation is emotionally charged enough so that you feel like running away, you want to engage in battle, or you are unable to act. Breathing becomes more difficult as you contract your energy. You begin to grasp for a way out. It can be difficult to get perspective in the midst of these situations, but it helps if you can get a time out or a momentary break when the intensity has subsided. Then you can reflect on what it is that you are actually afraid of. If the situation were to continue unchecked, what do you fear would happen?

Hypnosis, various forms of breathwork, and energetic healing are among the techniques that are most effective for accessing and reworking imprinted patterns.

Positive aspects of survival consciousness

The strength of the survival consciousness is the ability to cope in trying circumstances. Through the qualities of determination, resilience, and adaptability, you can learn ways to handle difficult situations. Later on, many of these troubling events turn out to be valuable for the wisdom that was gained.

Merely existing as an approach to life

While survival consciousness is effective for getting you through crisis situations, it is less effective and can be problematic in other situations. Engaging your survival consciousness when there is no true threat to your physical safety represents a distortion of the original intention. Your survival consciousness is based on an approach that once worked to help you out of a dangerous situation. However, it is only one way. The tunnel-vision focus dictated by survival consciousness can keep you locked into focusing on your fears, blinding you from noticing other possibilities. Coping is necessary at times, but merely existing is not the same as thriving and living fully. Just because a pattern is comfortable does not mean that it is serving your best interests.

Three

Security Consciousness

Security consciousness is a variation of survival consciousness that involves at least a little thinking about what is safe, whereas imprinted patterns are more like reflexive responses to perceived threats. Of course, there is some overlap. However, security consciousness extends beyond raw physical survival, as it includes financial and emotional security. Security consciousness is a defense that protects you from the intensity of a daily struggle for survival. It also allows you to avoid confronting troublesome situations and memories.

A basic form of security consciousness is helpful in maintaining a sense of stability. When your everyday needs are satisfied, then you do not have to worry about your survival, allowing you to focus on more productive and pleasurable activities. Crisis situations do occur, which may shift you into a temporary survival mode. However, the intention is not to spend your life trying to protect yourself against every possible future outcome. There is no way to truly guarantee your safety and health. Your task is simply to take care of yourself and to provide for a rainy day. Save for a rainy day, but don't spend every sunny day worrying about when the rain will come. Achieving stability is enough. The following descriptions will give you a sense of your level of functioning, helping you to assess how much of your energy is spent on security.

A healthy sense of stability

Financial independence is a big part of being stable in our culture. This means that your monthly bills are always covered, with some money left over for savings. You don't need to be a millionaire to be secure, but it helps to have a financial cushion and basic insurance as a safety net. You may be married or living with someone, but you could make arrangements to live alone if it suddenly became necessary. You may lock your doors at night, but security only becomes an issue during an unexpected crisis. You are usually calm and relaxed.

Strolling on the security treadmill

Security consciousness often comes to the forefront when you sense a threat related to losing your job, home, or a very close relationship. This is a natural reaction to these big life changes. However, for many people, these concerns are a common experience rather than the exception. If this is the case, then you may be on the *security treadmill*. This pattern is seen in living month-to-month, needing your next paycheck to cover your rent. You are barely able to cover your bills with no money saved for emergencies, accidents, or unforeseen costs. You may be dependent on someone else for your living situation. The difficulty of moving out and caring for yourself may be keeping you in place. You may often go from one shaky and dependent relationship to the next, fearing that you will be abandoned and alone. These patterns keep perpetuating a focus on security and leave you feeling anxious, worrying more than the average person. You may even cling to material possessions as a form of security. Some people who grew up during wartime or economic depressions may save all kinds of objects (that they may never use) out of fear that these items may become scarce again.

Jogging on the security treadmill

The treadmill has speeded up if you owe more money every month, getting into a pattern of debiting. Perhaps you keep having big expenses that were not part of your budget or you are between jobs for longer than you expected. You seem to be moving constantly from one apartment to the next. You may not have had a stable living situation for the past couple of years. Your relationships may be short, often with volatile endings. You constantly worry, to the point of being nervous, even when there is no obvious threat present. Fear of future troubles leads you to spend an enormous percentage of energy and money on security, while avoiding situations in which you are not in control. You may be fixated on security, hoarding material possessions, and setting up your home defenses with an approach similar to that used by survivalist groups.

Falling down on the security treadmill

A sign that you are heading for worse trouble is that you are having difficulty paying the interest on your debt and may be heading toward bankruptcy. You may be living with an abusive person or in an unsafe environment, such as being near gang violence. Every tough situation is perceived as an emergency. You may feel overwhelmed, helpless, panicky to the extent of being paranoid. You are obsessed with security, experiencing the world as a threatening and scary place, eventually becoming a slave to your survival fear.

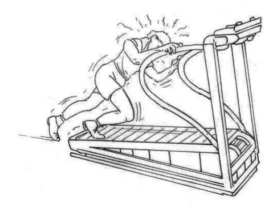

These descriptions are not absolute, as the lines can be blurred between the categories. An event can also cause a shift in your classification. While writing, I found myself strolling on the security treadmill, as I was spending the equity in my house, rather than adding any savings.

Your sense of security

- When do you focus most on security?
- How often do emergencies or crisis situations occur in your life?
- How often do you think about your physical safety?
- How safe do you feel when you are home at night?
- How many times have you moved in the last five years?
- How secure are you financially?
- Are you financially independent?
- Could you handle a major expense such as an illness, accident, or car repair without being in financial difficulty?
- If you lost your job, how long could you stay out of work without borrowing money?
- Do you have some form of safety net, such as insurance or savings?
- Do you hoard material possessions?
- Do you ever fear losing your partner?
- How secure do you feel in your relationship?
- How many partners have you had in the past five years?

- How often do you worry?
- How often do you focus on your fears?
- Do you let your fears stop you from doing the things that you love or trying new activities?

Physical safety

Any threat to your physical safety will demand immediate attention, as your survival mechanisms will override all other intentions. Very little conscious thought can take place until your personal safety is assured and the crisis has stabilized. In some situations, tranquilizers or anti-anxiety medications can serve as an aid in taking the edge off your fear (please consult a medical doctor if you feel that this is necessary). Even a temporary break from a crisis will allow your extreme fear to dissipate to the extent that other options can be evaluated.

Creating a safe living environment means getting away from dangerous or harmful situations. It also requires leaving anyone who is physically abusive to you and retreating to a distance where they are no longer a threat to you. For some people, it may be necessary to move into a shelter to get protection. Then you establish firm boundaries to ward off threatening people — lock your doors, get an alarm system, call the police when necessary, and strongly say *no* to destructive people and unwanted elements. This creates your own local comfort zone. From this secure space, you only allow those near you who are not threatening. In this way, root chakra boundaries regulate the physical space around you.

Reality check

Besides physical safety, the only other essential needs for survival are food, water, and the absence of life-threatening disease or severe mental illness. There are few people in the Western world who face true tests of survival in their daily life. While you may be acting from the belief that your survival is at stake, most people are dealing with issues related to physical comfort. The possible loss of these creature comforts is often distorted to be an actual threat to survival. I don't intend to minimize any difficulties or hardships that you might encounter in daily life, as no one likes doing without. However, I am suggesting that many people could benefit from a reality check:

- Will you die in the near future if your circumstances don't change?

Consider some of the most stressful situations in life: the loss of a job, home, spouse, or parents; major illness or chronic pain; physical abuse or conflict; or financial bankruptcy. These experiences commonly trigger imprints, engaging your survival patterns. While this reaction is understandable, the fact is that most of the situations just named are not truly life-threatening. Your life is not at stake, but rather the survival of your current identity. Knowing this does not make these challenges any more enjoyable, but gaining this perspective may lessen your immediate concerns and open up more options.

> *Security is mostly a superstition. It does not exist in nature, nor do the children of men as a whole experience it. Avoiding danger is no safer in the long run than outright exposure. Life is either a daring adventure or nothing.*
>
> Helen Keller

The role of fear

Ideally, fear serves a valuable role in alerting you to dangers and warning you of potential threats. Unfortunately, fear can be like the mythical Hydra monster, which grows two new heads when one is cut off. In this manner, a fearful thought can mushroom into a state of paranoia when it is given too much attention. Because your survival consciousness is based in the primitive part of the brain, it is the slowest to adjust to new information. Thus, many of your imprinted fears are no longer serving their original purpose and can become counterproductive. Indeed, many of your fears are not necessary, although it is important to stay alert and aware to potential threats. After an initial fear response, it can be beneficial to do another reality check:

- Am I truly threatened or is my fear excessive for the situation?

Facing your fears

When you run away from a situation, the resulting memory is that you are less than your fear. You overcome your fears by facing them. Like getting thrown from a horse and getting right back up on it again, your fears diminish when they are confronted. A first approach is to feel your fear and do the activity anyway. Almost always your fear of an event is greater than the actual difficulty of the act itself, once you attempt it. It can be helpful to ask yourself:

- What is the worst thing that can happen in this situation?
- Am I ready to handle whatever the next moment presents to me?
- If you can answer these questions, then you can courageously tackle the next task. Eventually, your fears become so trivial that you can dismiss them.
- Occasionally, your courage is not strong enough to confront a fear directly. It may need to become angry at yourself to provide the energy necessary to get you over the hump and face your fear.
- What difficulties have you overcome?
- What fears have you confronted and worked through?

Other approaches to fear

Sometimes your fear of a situation is too great to confront immediately. You can then go deeper into the feeling and explore what it is that you truly fear. Remind yourself that fear signals that you are alive. Remind yourself that you are not dying, although it may feel like you are. After all, you are asking yourself to let go of a part of you that once helped you to survive. Remind yourself that the feared situation will not last forever. Even when your body is shaking uncontrollably, know that this too will pass. After you have felt your fear in a deeper way you can own it, instead of running from it. When you embrace your fear, by staying with your feeling while taking some deep breaths, you begin the process of coming into your power.

Fears can block your mental ability to see other options. Two questions may be helpful in shifting your perspective:

- How would you look differently at your current dilemma if you had just won the lottery?
- What would you do if you had no fear?

The first question engages your imagination to think outside of your current situation, without the constraints of stifling financial concerns. The second question often yields a different response, uncovering your true desires, identifying deeper fears, and quantifying that the risk is not so great.

As you grow and become more empowered, your capacity to handle people and problems becomes greater. Fears that were legitimate as a child may now be irrational. So rather than helping, your survival and security patterns can limit your sense of freedom and choice when threats are not as great as you perceive them to be. Without being conscious of your patterns, you continually repeat them and become ruled by your fears. In this way, proceeding as usual is an unconscious decision to continue your old survival patterns, shrinking away from the greatness of your higher potential. Again, there are no absolute guarantees for health and safety in this world. Trust life and know that eventually everything will be okay.

Four

Trust Issues

Your sense of safety and security will affect your degree of trust. If you experienced having a physically and emotionally secure infancy, then you developed trust in your parents. This trust later enabled you to take steps away from your parents, trusting that they would be there when you returned. This experience became your basis for trusting others and trusting the world enough to venture out as a separate self later in life.

If the opposite occurred and your parents were less reliable or perhaps even abusive, then you did not feel completely secure, making it more difficult for you to trust. Children who experience abuse learn to become their own protector — staying "on guard" and watching out for the next threat of attack. They learn to pick up clues related to the pattern of abuse, so that they can identify an early warning sign of when abuse might occur. For example, a child growing up with a physically abusive father might imprint cues that help him identify when his father is angry, so that the child has time to run, shrink his energy field, and hide when he hears the front door slamming. The child is not fully able to be himself, as he is occupied with his struggle for survival and trying to stay out of harm's way. Constantly being alert to threats translates into a state of vigilance that requires enormous amounts of energy, with the adrenal glands working nonstop. This situation cannot be maintained forever, as it is draining and leads to a state of exhaustion. The child is forced to cope with survival instead of learning to trust.

Children who grow up in wartime conditions also stay stuck in the mode of having to be on guard all the time. Similar to children who experienced being abused, they view the world as a dangerous and hostile environment because this was the perception of reality that was imprinted from their early experience. When basic trust has been violated and lost as a child, it can be difficult to regain. Fortunately, even abused children had moments when they could trust their parents or other people.

Difficulty in trusting others is just one part of the equation. You may be projecting distrust onto other people who are actually dependable — or they may not be trustworthy after all. It is also common to trust too much: trusting people who are unreliable, manipulative, or outright trying to cheat you. My trust issues play out a bit in each direction. I am generally a trusting person, but will tend to trust others too much, setting myself up for disappointment. Occasionally, an object may be missing in my house and I will quickly jump to accusing a friend of having taken the item (and even condemn him in my mind) before all the facts are in. I feel guilty and stupid when it turns out that I had just misplaced the item myself. To varying degrees, trust is an issue for everyone, as we are all required to discern who to trust. David Whyte quips that there have been "15 billion years of evolution and still we don't trust our next step."

Trust is an experience that gets built into a relationship when another person exhibits behavior that is dependable and consistent. For example, they show up on time and do what they say they are going to do. A common trap is to project the burden of trust onto the other person: "Don't you trust me?" When I am asked this question, my stock answer is, "I trust you to be yourself. When you show me behavior that I can depend on, I will trust you." Consider Aesop's fable about Scorpion and Frog:

Scorpion wanted to get across a river to the opposite bank, so he asked Frog for a ride on his back. Frog was skeptical and voiced, "I'm afraid that you will sting and kill me." Scorpion replied, "Don't you trust me? Think about it for a moment. If I sting you while you are carrying me across the river, you will sink and we will both die. Do you think that I would do that?" Frog acquiesced, "You've got a point. All right then. Get on my back." As they got halfway across the river,

Scorpion suddenly stung Frog for no apparent reason. As Frog became paralyzed and just before they drowned, he gasped, "Scorpion, why did you sting me and kill us both?" Scorpion replied, "Because it is my nature."

It is important to avoid engaging in intimate or business relationships with the "scorpions" of the world, knowing that eventually you will get stung. It is just their learned behavior and is usually not directed personally at you.

Infants develop trust by venturing out and returning to check in, then risking by going a little bit further. Similarly, I recommend increasing your trust by taking *baby steps*. Remember, no one is going to be there for you all the time, including your therapist. So please don't set yourself up for a fall with all-or-nothing thinking that expects a person to be 100% trustworthy. A metaphor that I like is to view trust like a bank account. The level of trust grows as you have experiences of being able to count on a person. Sometimes a person betrays you, making a big withdrawal from the trust account. After such a betrayal, it can be difficult to trust the person — and for good reason — but trust can be built up again over time, as consistent behavior begins to yield a positive balance in the trust account.

- Do you generally trust others?
- Do you trust too much?
- Are you a good judge of who is trustworthy?
- Are you reliable?
- Do you trust yourself enough to take intuitive risks?

Five

Grounding and Rootedness

Your sense of rootedness can be seen in the stability of your home environment, having a strong connection to your family and community, and consistent, long-lasting friendships. It is also demonstrated by handling your daily tasks in a practical and realistic manner and having your "feet on the ground." This is the long term result of being well-grounded.

Grounding is the experience of connecting to the earth plane — similar to a boat dropping an anchor. Plants connect to the earth through their roots in the ground. When a flower is cut from a plant, it loses its grounding and slowly begins to lose energy before dying. The same thing happens to the life force of humans when they lose their grounding: their vitality begins to diminish, resulting in being less able to complete physical tasks, while being more vulnerable to accidents and injuries.

Fear will cause you to lose your energetic grounding. The less fear you have, the more energy you can take in through your root chakra.

The importance of being grounded cannot be emphasized enough. Since grounding is primarily a physical experience, I strongly recommend that you do some kind of physical exercise that increases your grounding.

Grounding exercise

Be aware that for those of you who have experienced severe traumas or abuse in your life, this world has not always been a safe place. When you practice grounding, your fears of physical safety may begin to surface. This is often experienced as pronounced shaking in your legs (and perhaps in your whole body), as you begin to loosen energies that were once blocked. Unpleasant traumatic memories that were repressed may begin to surface, along with the associated emotions. If this occurs, it is best to re-experience these feelings in the presence of a trained psychotherapist, so as to not retraumatize yourself. You can be assured that you can stop the situation when it becomes too uncomfortable or frightening. This is empowering in itself, particularly when compared to the state of helplessness in which these situations were initially experienced. It is important to remember that the original threat is no longer present and that you are more capable of handling these experiences than you were as a child.

Begin with gentle stretches, especially focusing on the legs. This will begin to open up the flow of energy. While bending at the knees, spread your legs apart just a bit further than shoulder width (Figures 9 and 10). Next, visualize a cone opening downwards to the ground with the pointed top between your legs. Imagine that you are sending energy from the point between your legs toward the center of the earth. The earth is your home. Say "hello" to mother earth and hear her saying "hello" in return. Try to connect with the red-hot, molten lava at the core of the earth. As you do this for thirty seconds or more, you will begin to feel your body warm up and your legs may begin to shake a bit. A little physical shaking and some mild fear is normal. This lessens with practice. You may also notice enhanced blood circulation in your extremities. Continue to send energy to the center of the earth, as long as you sense that you can handle the experience. Begin by practicing for five minutes and extend this a little longer each day.

Grounding your body

Drumming is another activity that can help you to ground. Your root chakra energy will begin to resonate with the bass vibrations.

For physical exercises and nutrition that is grounding, see Chapter 13, "Physical Ways to Increase Your Root Chakra Energy."

People who are well grounded enjoy the variety of physical sensations that the world offers: smells, tastes, feelings, and all kinds of exciting experiences (like the rides in amusement parks). They have a vibrant zest for life and are comfortable in their bodies. Athletes are generally in touch with their bodies and are good examples of being physically well grounded. Very few people are completely grounded. It is possible to be fully grounded physically, while your emotions or thinking remain ungrounded.

Physical manifestation

An experience is grounded when it takes place in physical reality. For example, the idea of writing this book became grounded when the first copy was printed. Your ability to manifest your dreams involves several energy centers and is not the exclusive realm of your root chakra. However, your root chakra is responsible for the final step of manifesting a project in the physical world. For example, building a house begins with an idea which is translated into a blueprint. Then a more detailed plan is made for the timing of the construction. Finally, the actual physical manifestation or realization of the idea takes place when the cement is poured and the boards are hammered together. The ability to complete the last

Figure 9: Grounding exercise

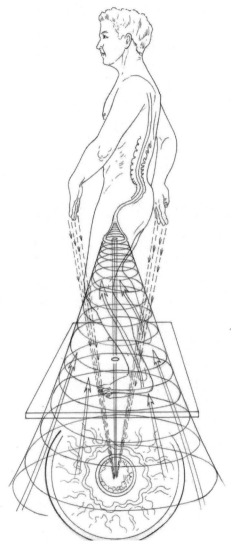

Figure 10: Grounding exercise

step of a project in the physical world requires the grounding energy of the root chakra.

If you have an inability to manifest your goals, this is evidence of a block in your root chakra energy. Examples of this are not showing up for work, missing big events, or projects that remain uncompleted. A large part of life is simply showing up for yourself. This may appear to be elementary, but it can sometimes be more difficult than it seems. It is much easier to avoid an event that is unpleasant. The reasons for not showing up are legion; in fact, I've added a few myself over the years. More severe blocks in your root chakra will result in your having trouble functioning and taking on the tasks of your daily life.

Some people attempt to ground themselves through their material possessions. This is a distortion in which you attach a sense of permanence to a physical possession and identify with it. Rather, the idea is to ground your own body and energy first so that you are ready to tackle your daily projects, eventually manifesting your dreams in the physical world. There is no reason to do without physical comfort and the enjoyment that various adult toys can provide. However, know that there is a fine line between enjoying possessions and becoming too attached and over identified with the physical world. You can check this by being aware of the degree to which you fear losing your material possessions. If you can let them go tomorrow, then you don't have a problem.

Orientation

As a child, you were dependent on your parents to guide you in the physical world. You began by orienting through your parents' experience. When they were present in the here and now — neither ruminating over the past nor worrying about the future — it allowed you to develop a sense of stability and to experience the world of physical reality with minimal bias. If they were not completely present or their own thoughts were distorted, it could have distorted your perception of reality.

Another common way in which your perception might have been distorted was by invalidating your experience, telling you that your experiences were not correct. "Oh, that was nothing" or "That was not important" are examples of such invalidating statements, in which a declaration is made about what you are thinking or feeling. When children are invalidated by their parents, they get confused and begin to doubt their experience.

Regardless of your history, it is important to validate your current experiences. Stay with your own sensations and feelings. Don't discount your experience simply because other people are not in agreement. Your experience of the world is your truth for the moment. This may not be the ultimate truth, but it is the basis from which you begin to orient yourself. If you have unusual perceptions, you can check out how your experience compares with the people around you. Then you can adjust your view of reality if it improves your sense of orientation and ability to navigate.

People who are not well-grounded tend to be spacy, distracted, or a bit confused. Their attention wanders. If you have a tendency to be spacy, it helps to focus extra attention on the physical activity that you are performing. You might even need a reminder, such as an hourly beeping watch, to bring your focus back into the present moment.

A gross fragmentation of root chakra energy is sometimes seen in children who experienced severe emotional traumas and is displayed in their difficulty with orientation in the physical world. In extreme cases, this can lead to schizophrenia, sociopathy, and pronounced borderline personality traits. Anti-psychotic medications can be a great aid in stabilizing these individuals, particularly in those instances when they have lost their sense of orientation.

How grounded are you?

- Do you have a stable environment?
- Are you practical and realistic?
- Are you comfortable in your body?
- Are you in touch with your body and its needs?
- Do you have good blood circulation in your hands and feet?
- Do you eat food containing protein?
- Do you like to exert yourself?

- Do you enjoy all kinds of physical sensations?
- Do you engage life enthusiastically?
- Do you carry out your goals?
- Do your projects get finished?
- How often do you cancel your plans?
- How often do you get sick?
- How well do you function on a daily basis?
- How attached are you to your possessions?
- Do you spend a lot of your time and energy acquiring possessions?
- Do you become overly upset when you lose something?
- How good is your sense of orientation and direction?
- Do you doubt your experiences?
- Are you spacy?
- Do you get distracted easily?
- Do you have perceptions that make you an "outsider"?

Six

Tribal Energy

Tribal energy is a form of survival energy that is extended to groups, so that survival of the group takes on the highest priority. The group provides safety for you in exchange for your yielding your personal power to the group.

Imagine what it would have been like to be part of a Stone Age tribe of nomadic hunters and gatherers. Each day represented a test of survival: providing physical safety from the weather and predators; acquiring enough food and water for sustenance; and coping with disease. Given these circumstances, almost all the energy of the tribe was focused on activities that might ensure their continued survival, thereby gaining a measure of control in a seemingly chaotic environment. Whatever worked led to group beliefs, rituals, customs, traditions, standards, and patterns of behavior. This is how various cultures were started, establishing a context for daily behavior and getting along with other members of your tribe, while at the same time generating a sense of belonging.

Over thousands of generations, these beliefs have become much more complicated and refined, although they are not always based on what was necessary for survival, but rather on what is considered to be "good for you." Some of these beliefs represent truths that have been tested over time, while other beliefs are distortions born out of misperceptions or patterns that are no longer relevant for the modern world.

Of course, we no longer live as part of nomadic tribes. Instead, we belong to families, clubs, local communities, groups with common interests, churches and religious organizations, as well as being part of nations and cultures.

Your groups or tribes

- Where were you raised?
- What is your ethnic heritage and religious background?
- To which groups do you belong?
- What are the characteristics or symbols of these groups?
- What are your customs, holiday traditions, or wedding rituals?
- How do you recognize other members of your group?

- Which groups do you define as "others" or outsiders?
- What characteristics make them different from your group?
- Are you aware of how many of your current choices are still determined and scripted by your group beliefs or rules?
- Are you concerned about what other people think and say about you?
- Do you make your own decisions or have you given your power over to an important person — a "tribal authority" — to decide for you?

In my workshops, I ask participants to identify three tribes to which they belong and to name a few characteristics that are associated with each tribe. While this seems simple enough, many participants have an unusually difficult time acknowledging the groups to which they belong and describing the typical behavior and symbols of their tribes. This common block in awareness occurs because many of these patterns are unconscious.

My tribes

Here are some examples of tribes to which I belong and some of their defining characteristics:

- Del Mar Starbuck's morning group — In the little village where I lived, a group of local residents gather to socialize while drinking their morning coffee. Although no one is excluded, a new person joins by sitting down at the table with a friend who already belongs to the group. The light conversation orients members to what is happening in their surroundings, as the talk is mostly about local gossip, events, and politics. Topics which are considered too serious or too emotional will be ridiculed, frowned upon, or at least not rewarded. If I sit down, I will join in the conversation. But if I am just passing by, I prefer to mention a few words about college sports, travels, or particulars of local events (i.e., the schedule for opening day at the Del Mar racetrack). The group will occasionally meet for barbeques, but many of the members do not socialize together outside of the local Starbuck's setting.

- San Diego North County New Consciousness — A loose association of like-minded people, who often gather at weekend events. Members have an interest in spiritual development with no particular dogma, although there is an emphasis on positive and cosmic energy, loving compassion, and creativity. Yuppies would not be excluded, but their value system might clash with the easy-going, hippie-like acceptance that is prevalent. Members must also be able to speak the *lingo*, understanding phrases like, "Go with the flow" and "That doesn't work for me." Some sects of this tribe (to which I do not belong) are vegan, "anti-ego," and into crystals.

- Counselors, therapists, and healers — A touchy-feely, groovy professional group. Personal growth is so important that it has become a committed lifestyle and a service-oriented career. Membership requires a willingness to listen to and sort out almost any problematic situation. Members who are not open to feedback are viewed as being unaware or charlatans.

- University of Michigan — We like our maize-and-blue teams to win (and to excel in academics). The winged football helmet, "Hail to the Victors" fight song, block M, and stadium are cherished symbols and traditions. When Michigan wins, I enjoy a little emotional boost. When Michigan loses, I lose a little energy. It is common to ride the fortunes of your tribe, like following a stock.

- USA — I am a citizen by birth, though you can also become a citizen through the process of naturalization, in which case you are required to pledge your allegiance to the country. The Stars and Stripes, the Statue of Liberty, the Declaration of Independence, and the Bill of Rights are important symbols of a nation that loves freedom, independence, and fair play. I also associate my multi-ethnic country with capitalism and a "can do" attitude. We are the strongest financial and military power in the world. We love it when our athletes win events at the Olympics. Yet, we are champions of the underdog and are willing to provide an opportunity for those who are willing to work. Is your view of the American tribe different from mine?

- Danish Viking — This is my ethnic heritage and part of my cultural background, as both of my parents are from Denmark. The strongest Danish symbol is the red and white flag called Dannebro. The Danes love to cultivate a quaint, cozy, and jovial atmosphere — epitomized by the Tivoli amusement park — called "hyggelig" (there is no direct translation to English). It is difficult for outsiders and immigrants to join into this Danish tradition because it involves a lifetime of socialization, plus the Danish language is tough to pronounce. Most Danes are non-practicing Lutheran Protestants. Their indoctrination is displayed during Christmas, weddings, and baptism, during which they take part in rituals that they have learned by rote, with little reflection or awareness. Denmark is a liberal social democracy, which has a "safety net" for those people who cannot take care of themselves (either temporarily or permanently). Many of their customs are built around "Jante's law," which loosely says that "you should never think that you are special." I don't agree with this creed, which clashes with the beliefs of my American tribe.

- Family — I am related to my extended family by birth, adoption, and marriage. This tribe has a strong pull during the Christmas holidays. I will share more about the patterns of my nuclear family in my second book, although I want to mention that one of our tribal beliefs is to create something special and beautiful. We were also encouraged to own or build a house.

- Spiritual family — Group of my closest friends with whom I share holidays and birthdays. We share a greater similarity of spiritual beliefs than I do with my birth family.

How tribal programming determines your behavior

Each of these tribes (groups) exerts influence on its members through beliefs, standards, and rules. Whenever you make a choice according to the beliefs, standards, or rules of a group to which you belong, you are almost always making a root chakra choice. In other words, tribal energy is displayed in behavior that changes according to the social occasion. For example, you would not act the same way at a funeral as you would at a football game after your team scored a touchdown. Although you may think that you are your own person and are beyond group influence, many of your behaviors are situationally sanctioned. The culture of ancient Greece was very permissive of men having homosexual relationships with adolescent boys. However, this is taboo in America (with other cultures having even more severe punishment for this behavior). Many American soldiers used strong drugs during the Vietnam war and were not ostracized because it was considered a way of coping with a difficult situation. Despite studies showing how addictive these substances can be, about 90 percent of these veterans never touched strong drugs after returning to the United States. These examples demonstrate how powerful tribal programming can be in determining your behavior.

Tribal beliefs can be difficult to uncover because they are often unconscious and are supported by the people around you. Gaining awareness of these patterns requires introspection and sometimes an objective third party, such as a therapist. If you aren't aware of your tribal programming, then you can't make fully conscious choices and your behavior will be managed by your tribe's customs, traditions, and rules.

Differences among tribal beliefs can result in misunderstandings, culture clash, or all-out war. These differences occur in situations where you have strong, preconceived ideas of *how things are done*. You are on autopilot, following your tribal traditions.

But when a conflict arises, it brings your tribal belief into focus. At this point, you have the option of blindly and stubbornly going forward or viewing the situation as an opportunity to reflect and evaluate the validity of your belief.

For example, I once was engaged briefly to a woman who did not appear to have any religious ties. However, she had been raised in the Mormon faith and these tribal beliefs came to the surface in the course of the early stages of planning for the wedding. Although she had not been a practicing Mormon churchgoer, the tribal beliefs were still deeply ingrained: marriage was a tribal rite of passage within the church, which was ideally meant to last for "eternity" and not just be a commitment for this lifetime. My tribal background from Denmark was that close couples often decided to live together for many years, sorting out issues as they occurred, and getting married as a formality (sometimes years after having children together). Our tribal differences, which were not apparent when we dated, led to many misunderstandings. Concerns about the wedding reception — her family didn't drink alcohol, mine partied like Vikings invading a new shoreline — became the least of our problems and we never got married.

Belonging to a tribe and becoming initiated

You can belong to a tribe by circumstances of birth, geographic location, profession, or for many other reasons. Joining a tribe often involves learning the traditions and rules of the group, being tested by an ordeal or having to go through rituals or rites of passage, and becoming physically marked or wearing a symbol of your tribe. Gangs are an obvious example. However, almost all tribes have ways of initiating their members. The tougher the initiation, the stronger the group bond becomes within the tribe.

- How have you been initiated into your tribes?
- What kinds of ordeals or rites of passage have you been through?
- What kind of schooling have you completed?

Positive aspects of tribal energy

Ideally, there is a mutual exchange and you get something from your tribe or group in exchange for your contribution to the group. Other positive aspects of tribal energy include developing a sense of belonging, loyalty, respect for your tribal heritage, and social skills. In most cultures, socialization is an ongoing part of the initiatory process. From an early age, children learn their tribal beliefs and rituals, which then become internalized as part of their deeply rooted programming. Socialization enables us to get along with other people and gain acceptance. Learning social skills includes basic consideration, such as greeting rituals, how close you can stand to another person, how loud to talk, etc. These may seem like simple skills, but there are complex nuances to cultural programming. Many tribes have very specific codes of behavior. The people who master these social cues have much easier and more productive lives, both personally and professionally. Conversely, those who lack social skills often have great difficulties that go beyond intimate relationships. Even everyday interactions can be emotionally challenging and can result in the painful condition of loneliness.

Belonging and group pressure

Humans are pack animals, so it is natural for a person to desire to be part of a group. While acknowledging this human need to belong, it is not necessary to give away your personal power to any group. Unless you are physically dependent on a group for food, shelter, or health, you have a choice about whether or not to follow. Examples would include children, homeless individuals in brutal weather, and people who are physically or mentally unable to care for themselves. However, for adults, these situations are the exception.

Being ostracized or punished are the two primary methods used by groups to get their members to conform and to maintain the power of the tribe. The fear of being thrown out of the group or excluded from activities is so great that the vast majority never question group rules or tribal beliefs. The second fear, of being punished by society for one's behavior, is almost as powerful. We all perform an intricate dance in which we balance conforming to social norms versus doing as we please. If you conform completely, then your personal spirit is crushed. If you do not care at all about other people, then you become a sociopath. Neither extreme is desirable. The important question is: How much do you have to compromise yourself in order to gain acceptance by the group? Society's not allowing you to shout "Fire!" in a movie theater will not affect your soul's evolution. However, not voicing your true feelings at a family gathering may keep you from claiming the fullness of your personal power.

Group fears

Almost all tribal beliefs were founded with the intention of teaching members how to live according to lessons learned from the past. Some of these lessons are useful and valuable, but many other beliefs are no longer relevant to the modern world and do not serve their original intent. If the basis for a group belief was a fear of some event in the past, this belief may no longer be serving you. Group fears fall into three basic categories: superstitions; racism or cultural stereotyping; and limiting beliefs.

Like an iceberg which is only ten percent exposed, with the largest part of its mass remaining unseen, most of these group fears are unconscious and are woven into the fabric of culture. For example, a superstition that I maintain is knocking on wood when I'm reminded that something is going well, fearing that if I don't, my good fortune will be taken away from me. The ritual is actually based on the idea that knocking on wood brings to mind Jesus Christ on the cross and invokes his spirit. The belief is that if I stand behind Jesus, then I will be protected from evil. I'm aware of this and I still repeat this behavior, though I don't believe in the same concepts of evil on which this ritual was founded.

Racism is generally based on fear of the "other" — a fear of the unknown — which can lead to cultural stereotyping, prejudice, and misplaced hatred. This is the true shadow side of tribal energy. Volumes have been written on this topic. I would like to briefly mention a subtle form of racism that takes place when we make a choice solely on the basis of familiarity. Although there may be no conscious intent to exclude other groups of people, this behavior continues the status quo with its built-in biases in favor of our own tribe and prevents a fair evaluation of other people and options.

Limiting beliefs are group rules or unconscious traditions that keep you from attempting something, especially a new activity. Examples include: don't question authority or you'll be punished; don't speak out or you'll be ostracized; don't draw attention to yourself because you're not special. These beliefs may seem trivial if they don't hold any power over you. However, the limiting beliefs that are relevant to you may only come to light when you would like to try something new — and yet you stop yourself.

- Do you have a tribal belief that prevents you from attempting an activity?
- Can you identify a specific fear in a given situation?
- Is the danger still present?
- Is the danger of physical harm real or imagined?
- Have you or anything related to the fear changed in any way?
- Do you have an increased capacity to confront and/or embrace what was previously feared?

By running away from situations that remind you of what was feared in the past, you hide and shrink from life. In other words, you give up on current situations without making an attempt to overcome the fear. By doing this, you are giving away your personal power to whatever was feared by the group in the past. Fear becomes the master of your life, controlling the way you make your choices.

Letting the group decide for you

In the same way, by deferring to the group rules without thinking, you are giving away choice and personal power. What is the payoff? You don't have to be responsible and you stay dependent on the group to take care of you. Because choices are governed by your tribe, the responsibility at this level is simply to obey family and community rules. The family and community system get the blame when situations don't turn out as you expected.

Doing what your tribe dictates seems fine when events proceed as planned. There is structure, order, and everyone has a role. Why buck the system when it is going smoothly? The problem occurs when the group system has flaws or when it collapses. Often someone who has been following all the group rules is now left with the short end of the stick. He feels let down, abandoned, and victimized by the process. Have you ever felt victimized because you followed the group rules, only to have the system not work for you?

For example, a worker has held a job at the same company for a long time. One day the business goes bankrupt and he has difficulty getting another job. Because the worker had become dependent on the company for a living, now he feels like he is the victim of management's decisions. He had given his power to the company, along with his daily choice of how to provide financially for himself. In effect, he made a bad bet and this was the consequence. Compare this to an entrepreneur, who must rely on his own decisions, with his financial future at risk every day.

Or maybe you belong to a Health Maintenance Organization (HMO). A job with this kind of medical benefit is nice, since unexpected costs are covered when emergencies occur. But you may assume that, once you have such benefits, your HMO will take care of your health. Then one day, you encounter a medical problem and expect your HMO will cure you. The HMO does its best, but may not be able to bring you back to your previous state of health. Then you feel victimized because you had given complete responsibility for your health over to the system and it did not meet your expectations.

Going your own way

Although situations like these may present temporary hardships, they can be a blessing in disguise, since they may signal a wake-up call for you to claim your personal power. Progress begins when you are less caught up in what other people might think or say about you. You begin to shift away from an all-or-nothing mentality, seeing that behaviors are neither good or bad, but that there is room for personal judgment. This contrasts with making determinations based on what a tribal authority has said is good or bad. Ultimately, you declare that tribal beliefs do not rule your life. You must also be willing to take personal responsibility for all your choices. Give yourself permission to follow your heart.

America was founded on the belief that we have the right to "life, liberty, and the pursuit of happiness." The key point is that we have the right to *pursue* happiness — we are not *guaranteed* happiness.

Happiness and how to pursue it is your choice; it is not the tribe's responsibility to provide it for you.

The power of language

One powerful way to break free from tribal or group thought is to change your language. The biggest shift is the simple change to owning your thoughts and feelings by using the "I" pronoun instead of the more familiar "you." Such "I statements" indicate clearly that your thoughts and feelings are yours. In contrast, "you statements" may be personal statements, projections, or generalizations. I often question people who use "you statements" for clarification: "Are you referring to yourself or speaking in general terms?" This offers the other person an opportunity to own his experience. It also allows me to challenge the generalization (or projection), so that the person knows when my thoughts and feelings are different from the rest of the group.

For more information about Tribal Energy, I can highly recommend Carolyn Myss' book *Anatomy of the Spirit*, as well as all her audio tapes and compact disc recordings. These were the source for some of my thoughts on this topic and have been used with her permission.

Seven

Only One Choice Perceived

Given the focus on following group rules and survival patterns, it is easy to understand that individual freedom is very limited when operating from the root chakra. If you are truly stuck in this mode and not able to access the energy of the other chakras, then it will be difficult for you to perceive any other options. You will hold the perspective that you have only one choice and that this choice is absolutely necessary. If someone were to question your choice, you might give them a reflex response such as, "It's the only way." You may even believe that you have no choice in a particular situation, denying that other options even exist. While there are always other possibilities, you may rarely acknowledge or consider them. When other options are presented to you, they are usually pushed away or quickly dismissed without being evaluated, as you may be locked into a particular choice already. This is often a sign of a sensitive and highly defended area for you.

Victim consciousness

Just noticing that you can see only one choice in a situation — or that you are experiencing no choice — is enough to identify that you are operating from victim consciousness. In this state of mind, you will often say that others have the power and are to blame, while events happen *to me*. All the power of decision is given to group influence or run by unconscious programming, so you own very little sense of responsibility.

Breaking the pattern

The first step out of this stuck position is to acknowledge that you have a choice, coming out of denial to recognize that you are making a choice in every situation, even if you aren't fully aware of it.

You may have tremendous resistance to this concept and defend your position. It may help to know that the choice you are making is not being questioned, so much as awareness is being brought to the fact that you are making a decision — even if other options do not appear to be viable. Beliefs like "there is no choice" or "this is the only choice" limit your ability to act and thereby lessen your personal power.

The second step is to recognize that more than one option exists in every situation, no matter how absurd the other options may be. For instance, you can speak your truth, even if you are certain that it would mean losing your job, home, or close relationship.

There are always other jobs, living situations, and relationships — no matter how unpleasant, awful, distasteful, or improbable you view these options. There is always another choice!

Eight

Self-Worth, Deserving, and the Will to Live

As survival is the main theme, your will to live — to bring your personal spirit into this world — is played out through your root chakra energy. I believe that being born is the first step in asserting your will to live. You choose to live every day, though this is almost a completely unconscious process. The opposite choice is to commit suicide. On the surface, this choice may seem trivial or absurd. However, it is common to fear both dying and wholeheartedly engaging life. The vast majority of people live somewhere in-between, a halfway compromise, not choosing to live to the fullest.

A baby's birth may be enthusiastically welcomed or not wanted at all. It is not uncommon for a bit of ambivalence to exist in a parent's mind because of the demands that will be experienced in caring for the baby. As the infant asserts his will to live, he experiences varying degrees of being encouraged or hindered. "A fish only gets as big as its environment allows it" (Mutash). The bigger the aquarium, the bigger the fish may become. Similarly, the more an infant experiences being welcomed, safe, and nurtured, the more its spiritual and genetic potential will be allowed to unfold. This is a key dynamic and developmental theme that continues throughout life.

There was a subtle struggle for power between your will as a child and your parents' will. For example, you might have cried out when your parents wanted quiet. You had immediate needs that did not fit easily into your parents' agenda. When your will as a child was thwarted, threatened, or crushed, you may have been scared and held back your assertion, limited your energetic intake, and doubted your own sense of self-worth. This is the start of self-limiting beliefs. A low sense of self-worth often shows up later in life as an issue of deserving or not feeling good enough. Almost everyone has some kind of self-worth issue, although you might not be conscious of how it plays out in your life.

You are a Child of God

Our deepest fear is not that we are inadequate.
Our deepest fear is that we are powerful beyond
measure.
It is our Light, not our darkness, that most
frightens us.
We ask ourselves, who am I to be brilliant,
gorgeous, talented, and fabulous?
Actually, who are you not to be?
You are a child of God.
Your playing small doesn't serve the world.
There's nothing enlightened about shrinking so
that other people won't feel insecure around you.
We were born to make manifest the glory of God
that is within us.
It's not just in some of us: it's in everyone.
And as we let our own Light shine,
we unconsciously give other people
permission to do the same.
As we are liberated from our own fear,
our presence automatically liberates others.
Marianne Williamson

From negative ten to zero

I believe that we are all children of God. Given this high pedigree, it is a sad predicament that any of us have self-worth issues or do not feel deserving of our birthright. To better understand this issue, picture that self-worth takes place on a scale from negative ten to zero (Dr. Tom Rusk). I like this scale, because all self-worth issues involve some kind of sense that you are *less than* or *not good enough*. At zero on the scale, your behavior is consistent with the statement, "I have just as much right to exist as anyone else — no less, no more."

At negative one, you have a few self-doubts that come and go. You may not return a meal at a restaurant, even if it is undercooked. At negative two, you may wonder if you deserve to be loved and get what you want. You have some bad habits that are self-limiting, such as often deferring to other people's choices. At negative three, you don't feel *good enough* to be loved just as you are. At negative four, you don't speak up when you are treated inconsiderately or disrespectfully. At negative five, you have self-sabotaging patterns. Some people are adrenaline junkies, repetitively engaging in dangerous, thrill-seeking activities that can be motivated either by unconscious self-destructive patterns or by the desire to feel alive. At negative six, you begin to display full-blown addictions. At negative seven, you have several self-destructive behaviors. At negative eight, your self- destructive patterns may lead you to purposely cut yourself. At negative nine, you attempt suicide. At negative ten, you experience so much self hatred that you commit suicide.

I want to make a distinction between self-worth and self-esteem. I define self-esteem to reflect how you *feel* about yourself (which will be covered in greater detail in my second book on the sacral chakra). You can feel

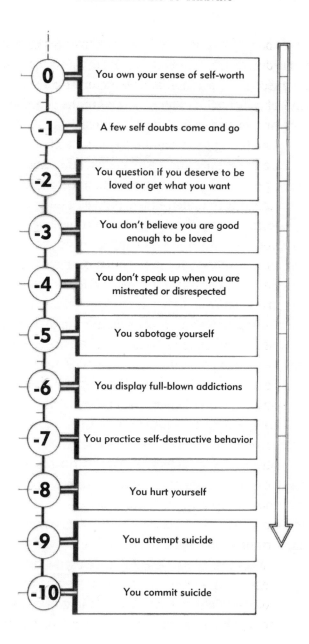

good about yourself and have positive self-esteem. This is different from self-worth. From this scale that I described, it is apparent that no one can have a positive sense of self-worth or believe that they are more worthy than anyone else. Consider getting in line for a movie or waiting for a counter to open at the post office. At zero on the scale, everyone has the same right to their place in line: first come, first served. No one deserves to be there more than anyone else — no more, no less. Do you believe this? What if a celebrity came while you were in line; would you let him or her go ahead of you? If you have an inflated sense of self-worth, believing that you deserve more than others, you are probably covering up an underlying negative self-worth. For example, if you rate your self-worth at a plus 2, you are likely covering up an actual negative 2 sense of self-worth (Dr. Tom Rusk).

Almost all people, when asked, say that they are deserving — and most people do believe this, in part. Yet your behavior may evidence that you are willing to accept less than equal, respectful, considerate, and loving treatment from others. Self-worth issues are often buried deep in your unconscious and can show up in many subtle ways. For example, when I wrote this book, there were times when I questioned if it was good enough. Beneath this doubt was a thought that I was not good enough, even though many people have praised both the ideas in my book and me.

It is often easiest to identify your self-worth issues by noticing situations in which you act differently than you ordinarily would. Another helpful clue is noticing situations in which you do not say anything although you are not being treated as well as others. For example, in my mind I have always thought that I was deserving of being with a beautiful woman. But sometimes I act differently when meeting an attractive woman, awkwardly stumbling in conversation in contrast to my normal comfort when speaking to strangers. Occasionally, I have even put up with less than respectful behavior, as deep down there is part of me that questions whether I deserve a beautiful partner. This pattern used to be more pronounced, but as I have worked on blocks to my self-worth, it comes up less often.

Your sense of self-worth

- Are your feelings just as important as other people's feelings?
- Do you deserve that other people pay attention and listen to you?
- Do you deserve consideration and respect?
- Do you deserve other people to be on time for you?
- Do you deserve good care or good service?
- Do you deserve to get what you pay for?
- Have you ever returned a restaurant meal that did not taste good?
- Do you deserve fair pay for your work?

- Are there any situations in which you are okay with getting less than others?
- Do you deserve to get what you want?
- Do you deserve love and nurturing?
- Do you deserve a special partner?
- Do you deserve the extraordinary?
- Do you stand up for yourself?
- When is it difficult to stand up for yourself?

Shrinking your energy versus standing up for yourself

If you limit yourself, it is because there are payoffs, such as:

- You will not be an imposition to others
- You will not threaten others
- You will not hurt others
- You will not draw attention to yourself

You shrink yourself, hoping that you do not get seen on life's radar screen, so that you will not have to deal with difficult situations. Any part of you that is negative or *not wanting to be here*, will drain your energy.

If you don't feel deserving, you will often give in to others and sometimes allow yourself to be walked on. Part of the task of changing this pattern is finding the place where you will stand up for yourself and say,

"Stop! This is my space!" It may take some will to fight back, but this type of courage does not involve bravery so much as it is an instinctual life-affirming power.

Shrinking my energy in order to cope

An incident that stands out for me as a child was a night that my parents hired a baby-sitter while we were in Denmark. Late at night, the Danish equivalent of the "Boston Strangler" came through an open window in my room and walked right past me while I was "asleep" in my bed. He attempted to rape our baby-sitter and re-opened a gash in her skull that had recently been stitched.

Actually, I have no conscious memory of what occurred, other than waking up some hours later to find our living room full of neighbors and reporters. I've always been a light sleeper, so it would be odd for me not to hear a person coming through my window. The situation was probably so scary that I woke up, played possum, and shrank my energy in the hope that the intruder would not hurt me. Then I repressed the overwhelming memory of the event. A few times a year, I still have dreams in which an intruder is suddenly standing in my room and I feel powerless to defend myself.

Shrinking my energy so that I did not draw the attention of a violent person was an approach that might have saved me as a child. However, as an adult, shrinking away from life's challenges is not an effective strategy.

The personal power of your root chakra

Actual life-threatening emergencies sometimes show the power of your root chakra energy to mobilize resources when needed. Examples of this include floods, fires, or major accidents. Such situations may require extreme measures necessary for survival. The result is that people often perform incredible feats, demonstrating strength, stamina, and courage not displayed in their everyday life. This is evidence of the tremendous energy that is available at the root chakra. This vital energy is potentially available all the time. The key to tapping into this energy is to wholeheartedly engage in each activity you attempt. A strong will to live is reflected in individuals with a vibrant vitality and a zest for life.

There are no guarantees in life. You could die at any moment from an accident or an unforeseen disease. Thus, many spiritual warriors vow to live life as if every moment is their last one. Generally, people do not realize how special it is just to be alive. Every person's birth into this world was the result of a tremendous success. Just look at the numbers. Something like only one in five billion sperm cells penetrates an egg cell and results in a successful birth. One in five billion! Every successful sperm is like a hundred-meter gold medalist in the Olympics (Gerry Spence). In my workshops, I try to substitute people's negative self-worth with that very image. I tell participants to picture themselves standing on the podium, having just won the hundred-meter gold medal in the Olympics, and ask, "What would I like to do next?" From this perspective, few people would feel that they were not good enough to approach their next task — that they weren't deserving or worthy. To anchor this experience, I give participants a medal just for having made it into this world. So, if no one has told you yet, let me be the first to congratulate you for having survived and made it this far in your life!

The personal power being expressed through your root chakra energy is demonstrated by your will to live. Every choice and action that you make in life symbolically states, "I exist." You can increase the strength of this energy by claiming and owning the following beliefs:

- I have a right to exist.
- I have a right to be safe.
- I have a right to have my own experiences in life.

These rights become the basis for claiming other rights further along the journey.

Nine

Nourishment, Getting Your Needs Met, and Having Enough

From conception through infancy, you were dependent on your mother for physical, emotional, and energetic nourishment. In general, if you received adequate nutrition and emotional nurturing as an infant, then your basic needs got met. You experienced getting enough. If you did not get enough attention, enough good quality nutrition, or your mother's breast was not available when you were hungry, then some basic need did not get met. You may have experienced a sense of lack or that life does not provide everything that you need. Attempting to fill this hole, it is common to respond by becoming overly needy.

The experience of lack or having enough is imprinted mentally and as an energetic pattern. This is reflected later on in life in the classic perception of seeing the glass as half-full or half-empty. This often becomes a self-fulfilling prophesy, as you unconsciously act on the basis of your perception. You may bring what you need into your life, thereby affirming that you have enough. Or you may push away what you sense is not adequate, thereby reinforcing your sense of lack.

If you were attacked as a child for your possessions, this can translate into a belief that "I'm not okay if I have too much." This can be seen in patterns of debiting, in which a person is unconsciously spending in order to "not have" (Gloria Arenson).

A sense of lack can show up in many areas of your life, although it is commonly manifested as a lack of financial security. When this becomes a pattern, it is termed *poverty consciousness*. Not having enough money only covers part of the definition of this term, as it extends to an overall sense of not having enough in life. The desperation of attempting to fill this emptiness is the root of many addictive patterns. Alternatively, you may overcompensate by hoarding material items in an attempt to avoid any experience of lack.

These early patterns can also show up in various eating disorders, as you can become anorexic by taking in too little food or you can become obese by overcompensating and taking in too much food.

- Was your mother available when you were hungry or needed attention?

- Were you breast-fed?
- Did you get enough?
- Are you more needy than the average person?

Real needs versus false needs

A person who wants a glass of milk should not sit in a pasture and wait for a cow to back up to him.

As a child, you were dependent on your parents to get your needs met. Being an adult changes this, as you can take care of yourself. Ignoring your needs will not make them go away. It can help to state your needs to other people because that increases the likelihood of getting some of your needs met. However, any real need that you may have, you can handle yourself. You are responsible for getting your needs met. Anything that you perceive as a need from a particular person is a projection and therefore a false need. False needs are usually demands for other people to be or act in a certain way (Eva Pierrakos). You can't make your friends or your parents behave differently, so pursuing this course is often a painful path. It may help to realize that your parents did their best, given their own childhood situations, to provide you with as much physical and emotional nourishment as they knew how to provide.

Two examples may help to clarify the difference between real needs and false needs. Physical affection is a real need. However, if you project your need for affection onto a *particular* person and believe it necessary for that person to meet your need, then you have created a false need. You have a real need to earn a living. Believing that you need a particular job is a false need.

Ten

The Language of Necessity: "Have to, Need to, or Must"

Your speech reflects your inner thoughts. Noticing that you are using the language of necessity — have to, need to, or must — is another clue that your root chakra energy is probably engaged. These words communicate the sense that there is only one choice and implies that grave consequences might result if you don't act accordingly.

Because our language is not exact, it is important to go a bit deeper and check this out. For example, it is part of common language to say: "I have to go to the store to buy a drink." This does not mean that you are truly dying of thirst. If asked, you might easily re-phrase your statement to: "I would like..." or "I want to go to the store to buy a drink." This may seem to be trivial, but your language can be a quick way to sig-nal that you are functioning from a root chakra per-spective. Since the root chakra focus is survival, the choices that are most often framed with the language of necessity are those related to money, work, or a very close relationship. For example:

"I have to check the stock market."
"I need to catch a plane for a business trip."
"I must call my partner."

Choices such as these usually do not get much reflection and, as long as the events turn out well, there may be little concern or second-guessing. When people are questioned about why they are using the language of necessity, a typical response is: "Of course, I don't *have to*, but I don't see any alternative, so I guess I still have to" or "I do *have to* work."

- Which activities do you *have to* do?
- What would happen if you don't follow through on a *have to* event?

The answer to the last two questions begins to access your root chakra imprints. Let's take a look at the example of trying to catch a flight for a business trip. If you are delayed by traffic on the way to the airport, you may begin to worry. As you get further behind schedule, you may start to feel desperate for ways to save minutes or seconds. You become fixated on catching your flight and your behavior becomes compulsive, as you don't perceive any other options.

If this situation were to continue unchecked and without reflection, it could escalate to a panic state, making it seem as if your life or death depended on the outcome. Your behavior is acting out unconscious programming that says, "If I miss that airplane, I will die." In this way, paying attention to situations in which you use the language of necessity can uncover some of your root chakra imprints. Of course, you will not die if you miss your plane. Your imprinted programming just makes it *seem* like you will die, as your fear overstates the actual threat.

Evaluating your fears

When you are in a crisis-like situation, it is a good idea to take a break and a deep breath in order to better discern your circumstances. The next step is to accurately evaluate your fear and your will to take on the challenge. Answering these questions will help you assess whether you are ready to take the next step forward.

- What is it that you specifically fear in the situation?
- Does your survival truly depend on this choice?
- Are you willing to take a risk?
- Does everyone else experience the same limitation as you do?

- Are you willing to take responsibility for your choice?
- Are you willing to suffer the consequences of your choice — even those results that are unforeseen?
- Would you be willing to take a very low-paying job if that was required?
- Would you be willing to live much less comfortably than usual?
- Would you be willing to be alone for however long it takes to find the right partner?

You may feel some temporary uneasiness, but few situations will require you to have to live uncomfortably forever because you address your fears. However, these tough questions often reveal where your blocks are and also your *willingness* to address them.

Many people take risks, but they do it in an unconscious manner. Then when the consequences hit home, they retreat into a safe hideout, blaming the situation or someone else for their choices. Moving forward requires taking responsibility for your own choices. The payoff for this big step is greater freedom and the right to live life on your own terms.

If you can disengage from a root chakra fixation, then you can up-level your perspective and move away from the language of necessity. Your speech will reflect your shift in perspective. More empowered alternatives include: "I feel like...; I want to...; I would love to...; I would prefer to...; I get to...; I intend to...; or perhaps we can..." You may notice that your interaction with others will also change and that options will open up that were not apparent before.

Eleven

Abandonment Patterns

The early experience of a consistent and emotionally nurturing bond between your parents and you as an infant was important in developing a sense of belonging. If you cried and didn't get a quick response, you experienced being alone and may have felt abandoned. You might also have felt abandoned if your parents were not fully present emotionally or neglectful in other ways. You do not have to be left on a doorstep in order to experience being abandoned. As a baby, you had no sense of time, so you may have feared being left alone forever, which may have led to a sense of desperation. These experiences of abandonment can be scary and are imprinted as part of your survival programming.

The consequences of childhood neglect are that you end up being overly needy as an adult. You may dread being alone, as it can bring up feelings of anxiety to the point of panic. It is common to have trust issues, fearing to be vulnerable and abandoned again.

Testing your way into a relationship

The hope is to avoid a repetition of your early experience. If this was your background, your adult relationships probably begin with high expectations and lots of unconscious testing of your potential partner.

This gets played out in several ways. You may wonder if a potential partner is willing to meet your many needs. Testing may begin slowly with an unusual request like, "Can you pick me up on the other side of town?" If he goes along with the request, you reward him with lots of praise and you may go out of your way to do a special favor in return. Thus, the bond between the two of you is strengthened. Then more demands are added as your connection grows. Part of this is natural in any relationship, but the subtle testing has a flavor of asking more than might ordinarily be expected. And if your request is turned down, then you may respond, "Well, I guess you just don't care that much about me." Such provocative statements test how much interest your potential partner has in you. It is common for you to frequently ask, "Do you really like me?" You may push to accelerate the pace of the courtship and sometimes threaten to go back to a past lover if you don't get a commitment. Your high degree of neediness is often paralleled with acting out some of your unconscious fears and anger by being unkind to a potential partner. In this way, you are testing how far can you push him before he begins to voice his disapproval.

Your unconscious testing will push less needy people away. This is the paradox of abandonment patterns: you have an intense need to connect with others, yet it is your neediness, constant testing, and fear of being abandoned that can push other people away. This is how abandonment patterns are re-created and continued.

Ultimately, you crave an intimate connection, but you are vulnerable to being abandoned when a potential partner sees all of your flaws, emotional wounds, and neediness. You don't trust that someone would love you just the way you are, so your testing behavior is unconsciously designed to produce a partner who will accept a relationship on your terms. But almost always, people who are drawn to you are playing out similar games with their own needs. If your matching energies are strong enough, you will tolerate each other's testing and end up with a codependent bond by plugging in to each other's needs. Ironically, rather than having the relationship on your own terms, you end up with one that becomes defined by your partner.

Energetic push-pull during your relationship

Similar to your childhood dependence on your parents, a relationship based on your root chakra energy is usually so strongly codependent that it may as well be classified as dependent. Because your early needs were not met, you will display the neediness of a child, clinging to your partner as a child would cling to his mother.

Your testing patterns commonly evolve to an intense energetic push-pull, with each person shouting: "Go away! No, don't ever leave me!" You know your partner will put up with manipulations like this because he has already put up with some of these behaviors as part of the testing phase. Additionally, you know that your partner is dependent on you for his needs. Yet, you experience uncertainty and have difficulty trusting. Based on your mutual fears of being abandoned, loyalty to each other takes on an importance that overshadows everything else. Few outside activities will be allowed to interfere with your primary dependent relationship. In extreme cases, only work and those activities which are deemed to be necessary for your survival are permitted. Other people may be perceived as a threat to your relationship, which often results in a loss of friends (who feel excluded). These characteristics are signs that your relationship has taken on an addictive quality. It may also revolve around other addictions.

Many emotionally charged situations can trigger your abandonment patterns, as you threaten to leave the relationship. Once these patterns and energies are engaged, a minor dispute can quickly evolve to an all-out battle for survival. Anxious and desperate behaviors are met with equally strong defenses.

Leaving your partner

Tragically, your fear of abandonment can result in behavior that escalates and eventually pushes your partner away. For example, telephone calls to check in and get reassurance may be repeated so often that they become tiring. Your lack of trust may be experienced by your partner as suffocating, as he responds by pulling away. This only increases your fear of being left alone and you become more needy. Caring for your insecurities and neediness may become burdensome to your partner, who may now wonder about staying in the relationship. This only confirms your original beliefs that you are not deserving of love, others do not care and are not to be trusted, and that you will be abandoned. You cannot see how your patterns have contributed to make your situation a self-fulfilling prophesy.

If you have abandonment issues, you will often run away and leave your partner before your partner can leave you, so that you won't have to experience being left.

Your relationship patterns

- Were your parents physically present for most of your childhood?
- Were your parents emotionally present or overly distracted by other issues?
- Are you more needy for attention than the average person?
- How comfortable are you being alone?

- Are you afraid that your intimate partner may leave you?
- Do you feel abandoned when your intimate relationships end?
- To what degree are you aware of testing potential partners?
- How secure are you when dating?
- Do you push for a commitment?
- How comfortable are you with yourself and your past?
- What aspect of yourself do you have difficulty sharing?
- Do you believe that you deserve to be loved?
- Do you experience being pushed and pulled in your relationships?
- Are you able to be in a relationship and still nurture other friendships?
- Do you often threaten to leave your partner?
- Do you trust your partner?
- Have you ever left a relationship because you were worried about being abandoned by the other person?
- What gives you a sense of belonging?
- Do you experience a greater sense of separation or belonging?

Working through abandonment issues

Your experiences of abandonment were based on your dependence on your parents for survival. As an adult, you are no longer truly dependent on any particular individual for survival. Remind yourself that adults may leave each other, but only children are abandoned. However, it is natural for you to feel abandoned when a lover leaves you, as it commonly triggers emotional imprints from your childhood experiences.

When your fears and anxieties are brought out in a safe space — such as a loving relationship or a therapeutic environment — then they can be addressed and healed. The basis for your desperate and grasping behavior can be owned as your fear of losing your partner. Reassurances can also be made that you care for each other, realizing that you will both be okay even if one of you chooses to leave the relationship. The testing behavior that pushes potential partners away can be changed so that you focus more on the qualities that you have in common. Your irrational fears can be evaluated mentally so that you do a reality check when you become aware that you are re-experiencing an old fear that has no basis in the present reality. Fears of being alone can be worked through so that you have a greater sense of belonging and are less needy. You can learn to express your needs without insisting that they get met immediately or becoming bent out of shape when people do not perform exactly as you would like. You can also learn to express your desire for physical intimacy without needing an ironclad guarantee from your lover.

The common thread in these situations is that the fear of an anticipated experience is greater than the actual fear when the situation occurs. I believe that at the core of all abandonment issues is an abandonment of your Higher Self, an abandonment of your faith. For example, occasionally I will pursue a relationship with a woman even though her behavior suggests yellow or red warning flags. In essence, I am abandoning part of myself — the part of me that knows better. As a byproduct of working through some of your abandonment fears, you may gain a faith that everything will be okay and that it is possible to trust that there are greater patterns or plans being played out perfectly — even if they make no sense to you right now.

Belonging

Each person is unique and has a different way of belonging in the world. No one can take your place and fill it exactly as you do. Again, humans are pack animals, so it is natural for us to want to belong and connect with others, as well as desire physical intimacy. None of us is perfect and each of us has been wounded. Somehow, the particular way in which you do not fit in becomes part of what defines you: the unique way in which part of you limps through life. This is the part you would often like to hide, putting your best foot forward first. But you cannot deny or hide your wounds forever. At some point, you no longer desire to hide this aspect, as your wounded parts call out to belong in whatever way they can. By defining and voicing exactly how you don't fit in, you begin to see how you *do* belong. When you engage the world fully — that is by showing up both with your strengths and weaknesses — there is a way in which the world comes to meet you (David Whyte). In that experience of fully meeting with the world, you learn how you belong. Thus, you find your identity and a name for yourself at the same time that you discover how you belong.

It is when you separate and take yourself out of a group that you no longer experience a sense of belonging. In reality, we all belong to many groups (no matter how distant other family members are), to our community, to our nation, to the world, and to Spirit. But if all that is too much for you to accept, know that you always belong to yourself.

Twelve

Physical Effects of Root Chakra Blocks

Root chakra energies affect your body via the adrenal gland, which affects your level of stress — and is directly tied to your fight, flight, or freeze defense mechanism. Your root chakra is further associated with your immune system, all of the bones of your skeletal system, and the area of your body beneath your pelvis — including your lower back, lower colon, rectum, legs, and feet. Like a slow flow of water that can erode the soil beneath it over a long period of time, energetic blocks will eventually distort cell tissue in your body and result in physical ailments in the associated areas. These maladies include:

- Immune system diseases
- Environmental sensitivities and related allergies
- Osteoporosis

- Chronic lower back pain
- Rectal and colon cancer
- Anorexia — not taking in enough
- Obesity — overcompensating and taking in too much

Disclaimer: This information is educational. It is not intended as a substitute for medical and psychiatric diagnosis or treatment where needed. Consult a qualified physician or get psychological counseling for assistance with significant problems.

Thirteen

Physical Ways to Increase Your Root Chakra Energy

A key to increasing your vitality and generating more life force energy is to engage life and be active. Deal with situations as they occur, evaluating them according to which activities increase or drain your energy. Disconnect from the situations or activities that lessen your energy. Your health depends upon making tough choices in these situations.

Physical exercise is a key component in boosting your root chakra energy. Stretching and walking are good places to start. However, true root chakra growth requires that you do some weight training using your legs and buttocks, with squats being particularly effective. I can also highly recommend the grounding exercise described in the earlier section titled "Grounding and Rootedness" (Chapter 5, p. 64).

Getting good nutrition is also important in increasing your root chakra energy. Foods that have lots of proteins, like meat, are necessary building blocks for a strong body and are naturally grounding. Make sure that you get enough calcium, iron, and other minerals for healthy bones.

Psychoactive chemicals that affect your root chakra energies would include anti-psychotic medications, sleeping pills, and tranquilizers. These substances lessen your level of anxiety and stress, reducing your sense of being overwhelmed. This is only a temporary mode of coping with troubling and disabling experiences so that you can function, but it is not a final solution. The original reason for ingesting these substances is often forgotten and the aid can then become a habit or an addiction. Unfortunately, a helpful crutch can become a way of life and a barrier to future healing.

Fourteen

Emotional Paths to Increase Your Root Chakra Energy

The emotions of fear and anxiety are central to survival and security consciousness. At the root of all fear is the fear of death, although you are probably more aware of your surface fears, such as worrying, fear of change, or re-experiencing a disturbing event. Varying degrees of fear and anxiety are displayed in panic, overwhelm, despair, and terror. Feeling helpless, lonely, and abandoned are also associated with your root chakra. Feeling one of these emotions is a good clue that you are experiencing an event from a root chakra perspective.

Growth at your root chakra comes from confronting your fears and anxieties. Throughout this book, I have detailed many of the ways that your fears can be identified: survival fears in crisis situations, security fears in your daily life, fears of being ostracized or punished by your groups and tribes, fear of being abandoned, and imprinted fears. As your fear decreases, you increase your ability to take in more energy and have a greater ability to manifest your dreams in the physical world.

Fifteen

Mental Approaches to Increase Your Root Chakra Energy

Your root chakra mentality helps you to survive and to cope with difficult situations, so it is wise to embrace this energy rather than avoid it. Most of your fears and beliefs were imprinted before you learned formal language skills, so your task as an adult is to evaluate your fears as they come up. Are your fears still relevant? Is this pattern still serving you? What would you do if you had no fear or had just won the lottery? The major goal is to break out of your fear-based survival patterns.

You also benefit by shifting away from all-or-nothing thinking, seeing that behaviors are not just good or bad, and that there is room for your personal discernment. This helps you to choose whether or not to continue following one of your group rules. This becomes a bigger issue when a tribal tradition conflicts with what you want or what you believe to be true. In line with this shift toward owning your personal power, you acknowledge that you are making choices, even if other alternatives don't appear to be viable. I strongly promote the use of *I statements* as a powerful tool in the process of claiming your right to exist, your right to be safe, and your right to have your own experiences in life — hopefully believing that you deserve just as much as the next person.

As an adult, you can choose to take on the task of re-parenting yourself, in which you make up for some of the development that you might have missed out on as a child, such as socialization skills or delayed gratification. Your mental ability is also used to sort out real needs from false needs, as well as to discern who is trustworthy.

Sixteen

Spiritual Aspects of Your Root Chakra

In order to better understand the spiritual perspective of the root chakra, picture a little child who sees his parents as God or gives them godlike attributes. Alternatively, imagine a caveman with limited understanding who attributes the cause of events to various surroundings, thus creating superstitions.

These examples show the limited sophistication of root chakra beliefs. It is common to let your tribal or cultural religion determine your behavior, such as following the rules of your church without questioning them. Whether it is just a remembrance to be nice to others on Christmas or a weekly meeting, any religion can serve to open up the door to your spirituality and remind you that there is something greater beyond your everyday identity. Given the human need for belonging, you may experience great comfort in finding a community of like-minded believers.

John Nelson

Root chakra prayers are often associated with critical situations in which you are desperate to survive a disease or accident. You may petition God that you (or someone close to you) be allowed to live longer.

Religions that are based on survival fears, or founded on a root chakra mentality, tend to emphasize God-fearing beliefs. However well-intended, these beliefs can thwart your personal growth by reinforcing fears and promoting a low sense of self-worth based on the belief that you are not inherently deserving. The characteristic all-or-nothing thinking of root chakra consciousness often leads to fundamentalist beliefs. These beliefs are overly rigid and carry the seeds of violence. For extremists, others must convert to similar beliefs or die. Radical Muslims are examples of this, as well as those who bomb abortion clinics.

Ethics

The *eat-or-be-eaten* ethic of survival consciousness is clear-cut, since you believe you are fighting for survival. Whatever is necessary for your survival is okay. An event that triggers one of your survival imprints can quickly bring this ethic to the forefront: whatever you perceive to be necessary for your survival is good; that which you fear or perceive as threatening is bad. There is little, if any, sense of justice at this level. Your tribe's way is considered just.

Shadow side

The shadow side of root chakra behavior is exhibited when you operate with an eat-or-be-eaten ethic, even when there is no true threat to your survival. Energetic blocks can result in barbaric behavior, evidenced by a willingness to kill, destroy, or go to great lengths to secure a small advantage that you deem necessary *for survival*. An example of this is road rage, in which you respond to a small affront by wanting to annihilate the other driver.

It is tragic to witness this cold-hearted, ruthless eat-or-be-eaten ethic, which can be present even in people who have lots of money. This is based on the distortion that material possessions are equated with security. In fact, no amount of possessions can guarantee your security, as there are very wealthy people who have other kinds of insecurities.

When your trust that *everything will be okay* is lost, your patience quickly gives way to emotional fixations in an attempt to restore a more familiar sense of perceived security. Then, when your compulsive behavior is challenged, that can often lead to threats and violent behavior to enforce your will and lessen your sense of vulnerability. If you fear change, this may be a typical way of responding for you.

The shadow side of root chakra behavior can also be witnessed in blindly conforming to tribal authority, believing that this absolves you from being accountable — defending yourself by saying, "I was only following orders." Racism, or viewing your own group as superior to another group of people, is another all-too-common shadow side of tribal energy.

Personal spirituality

At the root chakra, personal spirituality is grounded in a deep trust or faith — a sense that no matter how terrible circumstances may appear, everything will eventually turn out okay. This allows you to relax and be patient, even when situations are experienced as unpleasant. It can also free you from the eat-or-be-eaten ethic and the brutal behavior that can accompany it. This kind of faith gives you an inner sense of security, making you more open to change and less attached to your physical possessions. Group differences can be recognized without giving in to racism. Tribal authorities can be accepted for what they are, but you do not have to follow them with blind conformity.

Seventeen

Concluding Remarks

Since the energy of your root chakra is vital to the process of all physical experiences, it is clearly an energy to be developed and cultivated. Some of your root chakra blocks can be difficult to recognize at first glance because the patterns were imprinted before you could speak and are now unconscious. It may take a bit of focused detective work for you to become aware of your issues. Hopefully, this book has helped you to identify your root chakra challenges, as well as your strengths. Awareness is the first step toward making choices that increase your energy. By acknowledging that you always have a choice, you start to gain greater freedom and shed the bonds of victim consciousness. As you confront your fears and evaluate your tribal beliefs, you are journeying on the path from surviving to thriving.

The next book

The second book in this series, *Emotional Freedom: Reparenting Your Inner Child,* will be about your sacral chakra. There is a shift from the group energy of the root chakra to emphasizing one-on-one relationships: addressing codependence, guilt, obligation, caretaking, and various other manipulative patterns. As it is the center of your emotional and sexual energy, the variety of issues in the sacral chakra constitute a *soap opera smorgasbord* full of addictions, lying, revenge, and drama. The other side of your sacral chakra is the playful and creative energy of your Inner Child.

Learning how to set good boundaries and say "No" will be another major focus, along with working through your shame to achieve higher self-esteem. Another really juicy topic that I can tell you about right now is the partnered pattern of seduction-betrayal. Oops, gotta go. I'll tell you later. I promise. I won't let you down. I promise...

Summary Table

Energy: tribal
Consciousness: survival or security
Freedom: very little
Choice: only one choice (or a sense that there is no choice)
Responsibility: to obey family and community rules
Personal power: the will to live — "I exist" or "I have the right to exist"
Language used concerning choices: "have to, need to, or must"
Internal programming: "If I do not do this, I fear that I will die"
Informed by: imprinting that leads to drives, urges, and impulses
Issues:

- Safety and trust
- Grounding and rootedness
- Self-worth, deserving, and the will to live
- Getting or having enough: real needs versus false needs
- Abandonment patterns

Physical aspects:

- Vitality; ability to manifest and function in daily life
- Gland: adrenal — stress level and fight, flight, or freeze mechanism
- Connection to the body: immune system, all of your bones, the area beneath your pelvis — including lower back, lower colon, rectum, legs, and feet
- Diseases and disorders: problems related to the above areas of the body, allergies and environmental sensitivities, some immune system disorders, obesity or anorexia
- Chemicals used: tranquilizers, sleeping pills, and anti-psychotic medications
- Foods: red meat and proteins

Emotional aspects:

- Relationships: dependent, needy, and clinging
- Boundaries: physical safety
- Feelings and emotions: fear, anxiety, worry, panic, overwhelm, despair, terror, helpless, lonely, and abandoned
- Emotional disorders: schizophrenia, severe borderline personality, sociopaths, and seen later on in life as the regressed stage of Alzheimer's

Mental aspects:

- Minimal awareness, no reflection, all-or-nothing thinking, reptilian brain, learning via imprinting, pre-language, pre-operational, and rudimentary ego development

Spiritual aspects:

- Spiritual perspective: parents are God, superstitions, limited sophistication, God-fearing beliefs, fundamentalist beliefs
- Prayer: petitioning God that you or another be allowed to live longer
- Ethics: eat-or-be-eaten — it's good if it helps me survive
- Justice: little
- Shadow side: barbaric, violent, ruthless behavior, blindly following tribal authority, racism, and material possessions seen as security
- Personal spirituality: everything will eventually turn out okay

Major contributors and top resources

- John Nelson. *Healing the split.* SUNY Press: 1994.
- Caroline Myss. Anatomy of the spirit. Three Rivers Press: 1996
- ———. Energy anatomy & Advanced energy anatomy. Audio cassettes from Sounds True: 1996 – www.myss.com
- Marcela Flekalova: teacher/healer – www.schoolofhealership.com
- Bruce Sweatte: clairvoyant and hands-on-healer – thehealingsource@yahoo.com
- Victoria Merkle Center of Energy Medicine – www.victoriamerkle.com
- Gordon Merkle: licensed acupuncture, hands-on and energetic healer – (760) 753-2900
- Rosalyn Bruyere - Audio cassettes from: www.rosalynlbruyere.org
- Anodea Judith. *Eastern body, western mind.* Ten Speed Press: 1997.
- ———. *Wheels of life.* Llewellyn: 1987 – www.sacredcenters.com
- David Whyte – www.davidwhyte.com

Mark Lorentzen is available for private consultations as well as a keynote speaker for events related to personal growth.

Go to Mark's website to contact him or to find out more information about book signings, upcoming workshops, or future books:

www.allaboutchoice.net

Presentation topics:

- Chakras and the human energy field
- Working through your fears
- Abandonment, codependence, boundaries, and fair fighting
- Communication for better relationships
- Self-worth, self-esteem, self-respect, and self-love
- Claiming personal power
- Personal growth and corporate productivity